Learning C

(2nd Revised Edition)

Ramesh Bangia
B.Sc., Dip. Comp. Sc.
Formerly: Managing Editor, Software Today
Formerly: Incharge Computer Centre, Hindustan Copper Ltd., New Delhi

KHANNA BOOK PUBLISHING CO. PVT. LTD.

LEARNING C
Ramesh Bangia

ISBN: 9788187522546

First Edition: 2001
Second Edition : 2006
Reprint : 2007, 2008, 2009, 2010, **2011**

Published by:
KHANNA BOOK PUBLISHING CO. (P) LTD.
4C/4344, Ansari Road, Darya Ganj, New Delhi-110 002
Phone: 011-23244448 Telefax: 011-23244447
E-mail: contact@khannabooks.com
Website: www.khannabooks.com

Regd. Off: 1694-95, 1st Floor, Nai Sarak, Delhi-110006 (India)
Phone: 011-23283211 Telefax: 011-23256658

Printed in India by:
S.P.S. Printers & Binders, Delhi

Preface

Learning of a software is both easy and difficult. It depends upto what level you are planning to learn. If you are learning only for the working use, then it is very easy. But, when you try to go deep into it, then you realise how difficult it is to master it.

C is such a vast subject that it will take a lot of time to understand it fully. This book has been written in mind to make you aware of the options available in the software and how they can be used. It is like telling the child about the steps and stairs. You are the one who is to climb the stair. This book will just guide you how to use the stairs.

I am indeed debited to my publishers Khanna Book Publishing Co. Pvt. Ltd., specially Vivek and Puneet for their suggestions and encouragement given in producing this book.

I would like to thank my family specially my wife Sadhna, kids Mayank and Samarth, for without their criticism this book would not have seen the day.

Suggestions for improvement of the book are indeed welcome.

Ramesh Bangia

Contents

1 INTRODUCTION TO C

> C is still quite common though C++ is here. It is because of its flexibility to run on any machine whatsoever.

Introduction

C was developed in the early 1970s at Bell Labs, by Brian Kemingham and Dennis Ritchie. Ritchie with Ken Thompson had also developed Unix operating system.

Kenninghan and Richie developed C from another language called B, which in turn was derived from language called BPCL (a system programming language).

Developers of proprietary packaged software are very interested in C because it is considered more transportable than other languages. That is, it is relatively machine-independent.

A C program written for one type of computer can be run on another type with little or no modifications.

Learning Process of C

C language should be learned in the following phases.

Phase I: Alphabets, Digits and Special Symbols

Phase II: Constants, Variables and Keywords

Phase III: Instructions

Phase IV: Program

Let us read about them one by one.

Phase I: Alphabets, Digits and Special Symbols

Like all other programming languages, C also supports

alphabets	a to z
numerics	0 to 9

special characters	, . (*) etc.
white spaces	Blank space, horizontal tab, carriage return, new line, form feed, etc.
other characters	C can process any of the 256 ASCII characters as data or as literals

As you go through the language you will come to know which special characters C does not support.

Phase II: Constants, Variables and Keywords

Let us read them one by one.

Constants

C supports two type of constants.

Primary Constants

Secondary Constants

Let see how each one of them can be represented in C.

PRIMARY CONSTANTS

They in turn are of 3 types. They are:

Character constants

Integer constants

Real constants

Character Constants

A character constant is one or more characters enclosed in single quotes, as in 'z'. The rule for writing character constant is given below:

> A character constant in C must contain one or more characters and must be enclosed in quotation marks with both of them pointing towards left.

Integer Constants

Integer constants are whole numbers without any fractional part. The method of writing integer constants has been specified in the following rule.

An Integer constant must have at least one digit and must not contain any decimal point. It may contain either + or - sign. A number with no sign is assumed to be positive. Commas cannot appear in an integer constant. C allows three types of integer constants :

Decimal Integer constants (base 10)

An integer constant consisting of a sequence of digits is taken to be decimal integer constant unless it begins with 0 (digit zero). For instance, 1234, 41, +97, -17 are decimal integer constants.

Octal Integer constants (base 8)

A sequence of digits starting with 0 (digit zero) is taken to be an octal integer. For instance decimal integer 8 will be written as 010 as octal integer. For example, $8_{10} = 10_8$ and decimal integer 12 will be written as 014 as octal integer, for example $12_{10} = 14_8$.

Hexadecimal Integer Constants (base 16)

A sequence of digits preceded by 0x or 0X is taken to be an hexadecimal integer. For instance decimal 12 will be written as 0XC as hexadecimal integer.

Thus number 12 will be written either as 12 (as decimal), 014 (as octal) and 0XC (as hexadecimal).

Real Constants

They are often called floating constants. Real constants are numbers having fractional parts. These may be written in one of the two forms called fractional form or the exponent form.

A real constant in fraction form consists of signed or unsigned digits including a decimal point between digits. The rule for writing a real constant in fractional form is given below:

A real constant in fractional form must have at least one digit before a decimal point and at least one digit after the decimal point. It may also have either + or- sign preceding it. A real constant with no sign is assumed to be positive.

The following are valid real constants in fractional form

2.0, 17.5, -13.0, -0.00625

The following are invalid real constants

7	(No decimal point)
7.	(No digit after decimal point)
+ 17/2	(/-illegal symbol)
17,250.26.2	(Two decimal points)
17,250.262	(comma not allowed)

A real constant in exponent form consists of two parts: mantissa and exponent. For instance 5.8 can be written as 0.58×10^1 = 0.58 E01 where mantissa part is 0.58 (the part appearing before E) and exponent part is 1 (the part appearing after E). E01 represents 10^1. The rule for writing a real constant in exponent form is given below:

A real constant in exponent form has two parts: a mantissa and an exponent The mantissa : must be either an integer or a proper real constant.

The mantissa is followed by a letter E or e and the exponent. The exponent must be an integer.

The following are the valid real constants in exponent form:

152E05, 1.52E07, 0.1523E08, 152.0E08, 152E+8, 1520E04, E - 0.172E-3

The following are invalid real constants in exponent form

(i) 172.E5	(At least a digit must follow the decimal point)
(ii) 1.7E	(No digit specified for exponent)
(iii) 0.17E2.3	(Exponent cannot have fractional part)
(iv) 17,225E02	(No comma allowed)
(v) .25E-7	(No preceding digits before decimal point)

SECONDARY Constants

They in turn are of 5 types. They are:

Array constants

Pointer constants

Structure constants

Union constants

Enum constants etc.

Variables

These are the various names given to locations in the memory of the computer where different constants are stored. All the various types of constants discussed above can be stored there. Both name and type of constants are unique to that particular location. This means that you cannot have 2 variables with the same name or a variable name with different type of variables.

For a variable it is safe to have it of 8 characters though some compilers allow variable names of more than 8. Variable names must begin with an alphabet. No commas or blanks are allowed within a variable name, however, only symbol that you can use is the underscore (_). Next are the keywords.

C Keywords

There are as many as 32 keywords in C. Given below is the list of reserved words which obviously you cannot use in your programs. These are:

auto	break
case	char
const	continue
default	do
doble	else
enum	extem
float	far
for	goto
if	int
long	near
register	return
short	signed
static	struct
switch	typedef
union	unsigned
void	while

Phase III: Instructions

Instruction are nothing but the combinations of the above mentioned constants, variables and keywords. As we know from the definition of programming, which is:

Programming is a set of instructions given to the computer to perform.

In C we work under 4 set of instructions. They can be defined as follows:

Input/Output Instructions	These are used to perform the function of supplying input data to a program and obtaining the output results from it.
Arithmetic Instructions	These are used to perform arithmetic operations between constants and variables.
Type Declaration Instructions	These are used to declare the type of variables in a C program.
Control Instructions	These are used to control the sequence of execution of various statements in a C program.

Let us talk about one of them Arithmetic Instructions.

Arithmetic Instructions

Those of you who have worked in BASIC would remember that a computer instruction has two sides connected in between by a equal to sign (=).

The left hand side has a variable name and the right hand side has variable names and constants. These variables can be connected by arithmetic operators like + – * and /.

An arithmetic statement in C could be 3 types.

Integer Mode Arithmetic Statement

Here all the operands are either integer variables or integer constants. For example,

```
x = y + 2
```

Real Mode Arithmetic Statement

In this case all operands are either real constants or real variables. For example,

```
z = x * y
```

Mixed Mode Arithmetic Statement

Here some of the operands are integers and some of the operands are real. For example,

```
i = prin * rat * y / 100
```

Operations Hierarchy

Since we are dealing here with the various arithmetic operators. We must have the order of their execution.

If you remember that we had the following preferences in our maths class which was defined by BODMAS, as explained below:

B	Braces
O	Overhead
D	Divide
M	Multiply
A	Addition
S	Subtraction

In the case of C this is slightly different. Here we have the 3 levels of priorities.

They are:

1	*	Multiplication
	/	Division
	%	Modular Division
2	+	Addition
	–	Subtraction
3	=	Assignment

To show the importance of setting this order of execution, I give here an example. I remember that we in college use to test the knowledge of our colleagues by the following example,

2 + 3 * 4 + 5

If you use an ordinary calculator to get the result of this. You will get 25. Some guys even gave the answer of 45. But, if you apply the BODMAS method and operate the multiplication first then the answer would be 19, which is the correct answer. I have seen some scientific calculators giving this result.

2 STRUCTURES IN C

Each programming language has its own set of rules to work with the type of controls like decisions, loop and case.

Introduction

The structures in C can be understood in 3 levels, they are:

Decisions Control

- if statement,
- if — else statement,
- else if construct, and
- switch statement.

Loops Control

- for statement,
- while statement, and
- do — while statement.

Case Control

- break statement,
- continue statement, and
- goto statement.

Let us study them one by one.

Decision Control Structures

If this happens then I will do this else I will do something else. How many times you have faced this situations? Well, this forms the basic of our study of decision control structures. Here we will take care of statements like if this else this. First among this is the if statement.

If Statement

As mentioned above the if statement is used to test a query. If the query is true then some operation will be performed else the next operation. In its general form this can be written as:

If (the condition) is true

execute this

else

In C this is expressed in the form of a condition. But how to find true or false in C. For this relational operators allow us to compare two values to see whether they are equal to each other, unequal, or whether one is greater than the other.

Various comparisons can be made like this:

Comparison	*Example*	*Description*
equal	x == y	x is equal to y
not equal	x != y	x is not equal to y
less than	x < y	x is less than y
greater than	x > y	x is greater than y
less than or equal to	x <= y	x is less than or equal to y
greater than or equal to	x >= y	x is greater than or equal to y

Let us take this opportunity to write a small program to test the if statement.

Example: A tax of 2% is calculated on the interest received. If the interest on a sum calculated is more than Rs. 1000 then additional surcharge of Rs. 20 is added to the tax calculated.

```
/* Calculation of Tax
main()
{
        int = prin * rate * time / 100;
        tax = int * 2 /100;
        if tax > 1000;
            tax = tax + 20;
        printf ("Total tax collected = Rs. ",
        tax);
}
```

Here the interest (int) is calculated on the basis of principal (prin), rate of interest (rate) and the time period (time).

Once calculated it is checked if the same is more than 1000, if true then 20 is added to the tax, if not then it goes straight for printing.

Here we have not used the other part of the if statement, i.e., if this is not true then what? For this we use the following statement called, If-else, read on.

If-else Statement

This is quite similar to the above if statement. The only difference is that you have to define the next logical step also which is, what to do in the case the if statement is not true.

As a logical extension to the above program, we add that if the tax is not more than 1000 then add only Rs. 10 to the tax as surcharge.

Let us see how the program would look like now.

```
/* Calculation of Tax
main()
{
            int = prin * rate * time / 100;
            tax = int * 2 /100;
               if tax > 1000;
               {
                  tax = tax + 20;
               }
               else
               {
                  tax = tax + 10;
               }
            printf ("Total tax collected = Rs. ",
            tax);
}
```

In the above case if the tax is more than 1000, then 20 is added to the tax or the amount of 10 is added to the tax.

There can be various forms of if statements, some of them can be as follows:

```
if (condition)
            do this;
```

```
if  (condition)
{
        do this;
        and this;
}
```

```
if  (condition)
        do this;
else
        do this;
```

```
if  (condition)
{
        do this;
        and this;
}
else
{
        do this;
        and this;
}
```

```
if  (condition)
        do this;
else
{
        if  (condition)
            do this;
        else
        {
            do this;
            and this;
        }
}
```

```
if  (condition)
{
          if  (condition)
             do this;
          else
          {
             do this;
             and this;
          }
}
else
          do this;
```

else if statement

This is using el-if construct whose syntax is:

```
          if (condition-1)
             statement-block-1
          else if (condition-2)
             statement-block-2
          else if (condition-3)
             statement-block-3
                  :
                  :
          else if (condition-N)
             statement-block-N
          else
             statement-block-s
```

The condition are evaluated in order, and if any condition is true then the statement block associated with it is executed, and this terminates the whole chain.

The last else part handles the none of the above or default case where none of the specified conditions are satisfied.

The sequence of if statements is the most general way of writing a multi-way decision. The following program shows this.

```
/*program to demostrate the use of else-if
          construct
main()
```

```
{
        int day;
        printf("\nEnter day of week as
        number:");
        scanf("%d", &day);
        if(day == 0)
           printf("\nDay of week is Sunday\n");
        else if(day == 1)
           printf("\nDay of week is Monday\n";
        else if(day == 2)
           printf("\nDay of week is Tuesday\n";
        else if(day == 3)
           printf("\nDay of week is
        Wednesday\n";
        else if(day == 4)
           printf("\nDay of week is Thursday\n";
        else if(day == 5)
           printf("\nDay of week is Friday\n";
        else if(day == 6)
           printf("\nDay of week is Saturday\n";
        else
           printf("\nWrong input\n");
}
```

Switch Statement

It should be renamed as switch-case-default statement. These are the keywords that work together to execute this statement.

The general syntax for this can be as follows:

```
switch (integer expression)
{
    case constant 1:
        do this;
    case constant 2:
        do this;
    case constant 3:
        do this;
```

```
    default:
        do this;
}
```

This is how it is used. Well let us see how it is executed. First, the integer expression following the keywork switch is evaluated. The value it gives is then matched, one by one, against the constant values that follow the case statements.

When a match is found, the program executes the statements following that case, and all subsequent case and default statements as well. If no match is found with any of the case statements, only the statements following the default are executed.

Let us see the following example,

```
/* print numbers 1 to 20
main()
{
        int x = 1;
        switch (i)
        {
          case 1:
            printf ("It is case 1 \n")
          case 2:
            printf ("It is case 2 \n")
          case 3:
            printf ("It is case 3 \n")
          default:
            printf ("It is the default \n")
        }
}
```

The output of this would be:

```
It is case 1
It is case 2
It is case 3
It is default
```

A switch may occur within another but in practise it is not done. The switch statement is very useful while writing menu driven programs.

Using switch

This control statement allows you to make a decision from the number of choices. It is called a switch, or to be more precise, switch-case-default. It can be represented as:

```
switch ( integer expression )
{
            case constant 1:
               do this ;
            case constant 2 :
               do this ;
            case constant 3 :
               do this ;
            default :
               do this ;
}
```

Here the integer expression can be any valid expression of C which would yield an integer value. It could be an integer constant like 1, 2 or 3, or an expression that evaluates to an integer. The keyword case is followed by an integer of a character constant.

Each constant in each case must be different from all others. The "do this" lines in the above form of switch represent any valid C statement.

Let us see what this program does when it is run. Firstly, the integer expression is evaluated. This value is then matched, one by one, against the constant values that follow the case statements. When a match is found, the program executes the statements following that case and all subsequent case and default statements as well.

If no match is found with any of the case statements, only the statements following the default are executed.

Now, see the following program:

```
main()
{
            int i = 2;

            switch (i)
            {
               case 1 :
```

```
            printf ("This is case 1 \n");
        case 2 :
            printf ("This is case 2 \n");
        case 3 :
            printf ("This is case 3 \n");
        default :
            printf ("This is default \n");
}
}
```

The printout of this program would be:

```
This is case 2
This is case 3
This is default
```

Did you expect this result, well, I am sure you didn't. It has so happened that once the match has been found, all subsequent cases have been printed. This is why you see that all lines after the first one have been printed. If you want that only case 2 should be executed, it is upto you to get out of the control structure then and there by using a break statement.

The following example shows how this is done. Note that there is no need for a break statement after the default, since the control comes to the end anyway.

```
main()
{
        int i = 2;

        switch (i)
        {
            case 1 :
                printf ("This is case 1 \n");
                break ;
            case 2 :
                printf ("This is case 2 \n");
                break ;
            case 3 :
                printf ("This is case 3 \n");
                break ;
```

```
          default :
             printf ("This is default \n");
       }
}
```

The printout of this program would be:

This is case 2

Remember

You must remember the following before using the switch.

The above program used switch may give the wrong impression that it can be used only in ascending order, 1, 2, 3 and default. You can in fact put the cases in any order you please.

Here is an example of scrambled case order:

```
main()
{
       int i = 22;

       switch (i)
       {
          case 121 :
             printf ("This is case 121 \n");
             break ;
          case 7 :
             printf ("This is case 7 \n");
             break ;
          case 22 :
             printf ("This is case 22 \n");
             break ;
          default :
             printf ("This is default \n");
       }
}
```

The printout of this program would be:

This is case 22

You are also allowed to use char values in case and switch as shown in the following program:

```
main()
{
        char c = 'x';

        switch (c)
        {
          case 'v': :
             printf ("This is case v \n");
             break ;
          case 'a' :
             printf ("This is case a \n");
             break ;
          case 'x':
             printf ("This is case x \n");
             break ;
          default :
             printf ("This is default \n");
        }
}
```

The printout of this program would be:

This is case x

We can mix integer and character constants in different cases of a switch.

```
main()
{
        int c = 3;

        switch (c)
        {
          case 'v': :
             printf ("This is case v \n");
             break ;
          case 3 :
             printf ("This is case 3 \n");
             break ;
          case 12:
```

```
            printf ("This is case 12 \n");
            break ;
         default :
            printf ("This is default \n");
      }
}
```

Sometimes there may not be any statement is some of the cases in switch, but still they might turn out to be useful.

This is shown below with an example.

```
main()
{
      char ch ;

      printf ("Enter any of the alphabet a,
      b, or c");
      scanf ("%c", &ch) :)

      switch (ch)
      {
         case 'a':
         case 'A':
            printf ("a as in apple");
            break ;
         case 'b':
         case 'B' :
            printf ("b as in banana");
            break;
         case 'c':
         case 'C'
            printf ("c as in camel");
         break;
         default :
            printf   ("These   are   all
      alphabets");
      }
}
```

Here, we are making use of the fact that once a case is satisfied the control simply falls through the case till it doesn't encounter a break statement.

That is why if an alphabet a is entered the case 'a' is satisfied and since there are no statements to be executed in this case the control automatically reaches the next case i.e. case 'A' and executes all the statements in this case.

Loop Control Structures

In programming it is required to execute a set of instructions many times over. For this we store a set of instructions in a group and this group can be accessed any time.

For example if you are using a program where you need to convert a foreign currency to Indian Rupees. Obviously you would not like to use it every time you come across this. So what you do is, you store the instructions for this and call them whenever needed in the program.

This process is called Looping in C.

Loops

This involves repeating some portion of the program either a specified number of times or until a particular condition is being satisfied. This repetitive operation is done through a loop control structure.

There are 3 methods by way of which we can repeat a part of a program.

They are:

For loop
While loop
Do-while loop

Let us see how each of them works.

While Loop

The syntax for the while statement can be put as the following:

```
initialize loop counter;
    while (test loop counter using a condition)
    {
```

do this;

and this;

increment loop counter;

}

This can be explained by a simple program too.

```
/* print numbers 1 to 20
main()
{
        int x = 1;
        while (x <= 20);
        {
            printf  (x);
            x = x + 1;
        }
}
```

This is indeed a simple program where you keep on adding 1 to the value of x and then keep on printing it. Let us now see the other loop called the for loop.

The for Loop

The for statement is used to specify the following 3 things about a loop.

1. Setting a loop counter to an initial value.
2. Testing the loop counter to determine whether its value has reached the number of repetitions desired.
3. Increasing the value of loop counter each time the program segment within the loop has been executed.

Its syntax can be defined as following:

for (initialize counter; test counter; increment counter)

{

do this;

and this;

}

Let us apply this to our program and see what changes can be made in that.

```
/* print numbers 1 to 20
main()
{

        int x = 1;
        for (x = 1; x <= 20; x = x + 1);
        {
            printf (x);
        }
}
```

Let us try to analyze the above program. The for statement is executed for the first time, the value of x is set to an initial value of 1.

Obviously it is less than 20, so the body of the loop is executed for the first time.

Then on reaching the closing brace of for, computer sends the control back to the for statement, where the value of x gets incremented by 1.

Again the test is preformed and the same routine is performed. The moment is reaches the value of 20, it is end the loop.

The do-while Loop

Its syntax can be defined as following:

```
do
{
    this;
    and this;
    and this;
} while (this condition is true);
```

There is a minor difference between the working of while and do-while loops. This difference is the place where the condition is tested.

The while tests the condition before executing any of the statements within the while loop.

As against this, the do-while tests the condition after having executed the statements within the loop.

When applied this to our program the program will look like the following:

```
/* print numbers 1 to 20
main()
{

            int x = 1;
            do
            {
               printf (x);
            } while (x <= 20)
}
```

Of the various types of loop, it is the do-while loop which is very rarely used. The other ones are used very often.

Case Control Structures

These are used when you have to make a choice between a number of alternatives instead of only one or two.

In C you can handle these control statements with ease. They make the best use of the switch statement.

Let us study it in details.

break Statement

The break statement transfers the control out of the block where it is used.

Please remember that statement(s) enclosed in a pair of braces constitute a block.

The syntax break statement is

```
break;
```

The break statement is also used in conjunction with a for, a while, and a do — while statement.

goto Statement

This is one of those statements which you have to read for the reading sake. A good programmer would probably not use it for many reasons.

The main among this is the difficulty in debugging the same. A goto statement can cause program control to end up almost anywhere in the program.

Consider the following program.

```
main()
{
in goals ;

          printf ("Enter the number of runs scored
          by India");
          scanf ("%d", &runs);

          if ( runs <  = 250)
          goto sos;
          else
          {

            printf  ("This  is  the  right  time
          for\n");
            printf ("players to stop advertising
          and start playing");
            exit( )  ;  /*  terminates  program
          execution8/
          }

          sos:
          printf ("Its ok this time!");
}
```

And here are two sample runs of the program.....

```
Enter  the  number  of  runs  scored  by
India 268

Its ok this time!
```

```
Enter the number of runs scored by
India 180

This is the right time for

Players to stop advertising and start
playing
```

The only time you would probably be making the use of goto statement is when you want to take the control out of the loop which is contained in several other loops.

The following program illustrates this.

```
main()
{
int i, j, k;

        for (i = 1 ; i<=3;++)
        {
            for  (j=1,j<=3;j++)
            {
                for  (k=1; k<=3;++)
                {
                if  (i==3&&j==3&&k==3)
                    goto out;
                else
                    printf  (%d%d%d\n", I,j,k);
                }
            }
        }
out:
printf ("Out of the loop at last!");
)
```

Go through the program carefully and find out how it works. Also write down the same program without using goto.

continue Statement

In looping statements, sometimes a situation may arise where we want that from a given statement onwards the rest of the statements upto the last statement of the loop are to be bypassed.

This task is accomplished by using continue statement whose syntax is:

```
continue;
```

The continue statement transfers the control to the beginning of the loop, bypassing the statements which are not yet executed.

Consider the following segment:

```
    :
i = 0;
while(i <= 100)
    {
        ......
        if(i % 10 == 0)
            continue;
        ......
    }
        :
```

The use of continue statement in conjuction with if statement skips the rest of the statements of the while loop for values of i divisible by 10.

Exit From a Loop Statement

There are two ways to get out of a loop:

Normal Exit

A normal exit takes place when the loop's test condition fails. In such a case, control is transferred to the first executable statement following the loop statement.

Abnormal Exit

It is possible to transfer control from inside the body a loop to a statement immediately following the loop or somewhere else, even though the test condition is still true.

Such an exit is termed as abnormal exit.

3 FUNCTIONS AND POINTERS IN C

Software developers are generous. They give you a few ready made small program routine to work with.

Introduction

As your program increases in size and complexity, you should break them up into smaller more manageable pieces called functions. Each function within your program should perform a specific task. For example, if you are writing a financial program, there would be a function to decode your numeric figures to alpha figures, i.e., to write Rs. 853.67 to Rupees Eight Hundred Fifty Three and Paisa Sixty Seven only. It is like a program within a program. You would be surprised to know that C supports a lot of functions which are in-built into the program and you can use them at will by just calling them by their name.

The general syntax of the function can be:

```
function (arg1, arg2, arg3)
type arg1, arg2, arg3;
{
    statements 1;
    statements 2;
    statements 3;
}
```

Putting this into use we use the function called message() in the following program.

```
/* Print messages
main()
{
   message();
   printf ("This is the 2nd line of message");
}
message()
{
   printf ("This is the 1st line of message");
```

```
}
```

This will result in the following:

```
This is the 1st line of message
This is the 2nd line of message
```

If you look at the program you would notice that on encountering message() in the program the control has shifted to message() function and printed the line under it. The outer brace would send the control back to the place from it had come. On coming back it will execute the second print statement, which would result in the above messages being printed on the screen.

Thus, the function can be said to have the following options.

1. C program is a collection of one or more functions.
2. A function can be called when the name is followed by a semicolon (;). For example,

```
main()
{
    message()
}
```

3. A function can be defined by including the statement(s) within the two braces after its name. For example,

```
message()
{
    statement 1;
    statement 2;
}
```

4. You can call a function from within a function. For example,

```
message()
{
    statement 1;
    main();
}
```

5. A function can be called a number of times. For example,

```
main()
{
    message();
```

```
        message();
    }
    message()
    {
        printf("\nSachin Tendulkar");
    }
```

6. You can give the functions any name in the form of numbers and they need not be stored in that sequence. Program would look for the function name in the whole program.
7. A function can be called from other function, but a function cannot be defined in another function.

Types of Functions

There are two types of functions:

User defined functions

Library functions

The first one are those which you define yourself whereas the second ones are those which are available with the software. A complete list of functions is given in a later chapter. Let us now consider the various other aspects of functions.

Declaration in Functions

When a function is called upon to return a value it returns an integer value. In case you want it to return any other value, you would have to specifically mention it. A look at the following program would illustrate this point:

```
/* Print squares
main()
{
   float square()
   float x,y;
   printf ("\nEnter a number");
   scanf("%f", &a);
   b = square (a);
   printf ("\nSquare of %f is %f", x,y)
}
float square (float a)
```

```
{
    float b;
    b = a*a;
    return (b);
}
```

When you run this program you will get the following result.

Enter any number 5
Square of 5 is 25.000

Enter any number 7
Square of 7 is 49.000

Remember here that since we wanted the results in floating point that is why we gave the value in float. The function square() must be declared as float in main() as well for this. The statement float square() means that it is a function which will return a float value.

Recursion

A function is called recursive if a statement within the body of a function calls the same function. The following example will make it more clear.

```
/* Print factorial value
main()
{
    int x, fact;
    print ("\nEnter any number");
    scanf ("%d", &x);
    fact = factorial (x);
    printf ("Factorial value = %d", fact);
}
factorial(int a)
{
    int f = 1,i
    for (i=a; i>=1; i--)
        f=f*i;
    return(f);
}
```

This is what you will get on running this program.

Enter any number =   2
Factorial value = 2

Pointers and Indirection

Most programming languages use only static variables. Static in the sense that they are declared in the variable declaration block of the program and memory is allocated for them during compilation time. When the program is executing, the program can neither obtain more of these variables nor deallocate (i.e. free) the storage occupied by these variables. To access a value of such variables, we simply use the variable's name. The C language provides another approach which enables the program to acquire as much as storage required to storage more values and at the same time allow the program to deallocate the storage which is no more required by the program. This is accomplished through the use of special variables called pointer variables or simply pointers.

Pointers, by most people, are regarded as one of the most difficult topics in C. There are several reasons for this. For example

- The concept behind pointers – indirection – may be new one for many programmers, since it is not used in many languages, such as FORTRAN, BASIC etc.
- The symbols used for pointer notation in C are not as clear as they should be. For example, the same symbol '*' (asterisk) is used for two different but related purposes; once for declaring a pointer variable and then for accessing value pointed to by a pointer variable.

However, learning pointers may be difficult, but not too difficult. In an attempt to achieve our goal to learn about pointers, we ensure that the ground work is laid carefully before we go on to use pointers in more advanced situations.

What is a Pointer Variable?

In some situations, a more convenient and efficient way to access a variable is through second variable that holds the address of the first variable to be accessed. This second variable that holds the address of the first variable is called a pointer variable. Pointers provide a way of accessing a variable without referring to the variable directly.

Advantages of Using Pointers

Some of the advantages offered by the use of pointer are:

- to return more than one value from a function.
- to pass arrays and strings more efficiently as arguments to a function.
- to create complex data structures, such as linked lists, binary trees and graphs, where one data structure element must contain references to the other data structures of same type.
- to communicate with operating system about memory. For example, the function malloc() returns the location of free memory block by using a pointer and the function free() returns the memory block pointed to by a pointer to the operating system.
- the pointer notation compiles into faster and more efficient code.

Declaring a Pointer Variable

Like other variables, the pointer variables are to declared first in the declaration block to tell the compiler that to which kind of values these variables will be pointing. The syntax for declaring a pointer variables is

```
type  *pointer_variable_name:
```

where type is pre-defined or user-defined data types and indicates that the pointer will point to the variable of that specific data type and character '*' indicates that variable is a pointer variable.

For example, the statement

```
int *ptr;
```

declares a pointer variable of integer type i.e. pointer variable that will hold the address of storage location where integer value is stored or will be stored and sets asides a 2-byte space in memory for it.

The pointer variable(s) declaration can also be combined with the declaration of other variables, provided they are of same type. For example, the statement

```
int x, *px;
```

declares an integer variable x and a pointer variable px.

Please remember that a pointer variable must be appropriately intialized before it can be used. Otherwise, like other variables, it will take a garbage value, which can be a address of any storage location. Therefore, if not properly initialized a pointer may point to any location in memory including those where DOS is running and your system may hang-up, i.e., stop responding. Such un-initialized pointers are sometimes referred to as dangling pointers.

Accessing Values Using Pointers

To access a value pointed to by a pointer variable, the character '*' is prefixed with the pointer variable name, as is done in the pointer declaration. Here the character '*' is used as indirection operator as its allows to access the value of a variable indirectly. Please note that the character '*' in the declaration statement tells the compiler that value to be accessed is the value stored in storage location whose address is held in a pointer variable.

Consider the following statements

```
int *px, x = 10;
    :
px = &x;
    :
printf ( "value of variable x = %d\n",x);
printf ( "value of variable pointed to by px =
          %\n", *px);
printf ( "address of variable x = %\n", px);
    :
```

The declaration statement tells the compiler that px is pointer variable that will point to an integer value, x is an integer variable and it also initializes the variable x with value 10. And suppose that during the execution of the above segment, a memory location with address 1098 is set aside for variable x. The output of the above segment will look like:

```
value of variable x = 10
value of variable pointed to by px = 10
address of variable x = 1098
```

Types of Pointers

Based on the fact that whether a pointer variable holds the address of an address of an integer, a float, or a character variable, the pointers are classified as integer pointers, real pointers, character pointers and so on.

Pointer Arithmetic

The C language is very consistent in its approach to pointer arithmetic. The integration of pointers, arrays and pointer arithmetic is one of the strengths of the C language.

The following operations are permitted on pointers.

1. Addition of a number to a pointer variable.

   Suppose p is a pointer variable pointing to an element of integer type, then the statement

   ```
   p++;
   ```

   increments the value of p by a factor of 2, so that it points to the next location that holds another value of integer type. This increment will be 1 for character, 4 for long integer and float and 8 for long float. The statement

   ```
   p +=i;
   ```

   where i is either a positive integer constant or an integer variable having positive value, increments p such that it points to the ith location beyond the location to which it is currently pointing.

2. Subtraction of a number from a pointer variable.

   Suppose p is a pointer variable pointing to an element of integer type, then the statement

   ```
   p—;
   ```

   decrements the value of p by a factor of 2, so that it now points to the location preceding the current location. The statement

   ```
   p–=i;
   ```

   where i is either a positive integer constant or an integer variable having positive value, decrements p such that it points to the ith location before the location to which it is currently pointing.

3. Subtraction of one pointer variable form another.

   One pointer variable can be subtracted from another provided both point to the same data type. The difference of the two indicates the number of bytes separating the corresponding elements.

In addition to these arithmetic operations, the pointer variables can be compared with one another, provided they point to the same data type.

The following arithmetic operations on pointers are not permitted.

- Addition of two pointer variables.
- Multiplication of a pointer variable by a number.
- Division of a pointer variable by a number.

Pointer to a Pointer

A pointer is variable that holds the address of another variable. This concept can be further extended. We can have a variable that hold an address of a variable that in turn holds an address of another variable. This type of variable will be known as pointer to pointer. The underlying concept is known as double indirection. This concept can be further extended to triple level, fourth level, and so on.

A pointer to a pointer will be declared as

```
int**ptr;
```

The value pointed to by a pointer to another pointer will be accessed as

```
**ptr;
```

More About Pointers

In C compilers implemented on computers which are no built on Intel processors, the address held by a pointer variable is the physical (actual) address of a memory location. However, in C compilers implemented on Intel based processor, such as Turbo C, the situation is quite different. This is because of different memory management scheme with these processors.

The pointers in Turbo C can be classified as near, far, or huge pointers. To understand this classification, it is necessary to understand the memory management and addressing schemes of the PC's based on Intel 8086 family of processors and the various memory models supported by Turbo C compiler.

Near Pointers

To reference memory locations, there are two situations:

the referenced memory location is in a currently loaded segment and

- the referenced memory location is in an another segment.

To access any location within the currently loaded segment, only the offset address which is 16-bit address is required. This means that any memory location referenced using only 16-bit address must be within the currently loaded segment. This is referred to as a near address or a near pointer. A near occupies 2-types of memory.

Far Pointers

To access any location outside the currently loaded segment, both segment address and offset address, which after address calculation yields 20-bit address, is required. This is referred to as a far address or a far pointer. A far pointer occupies 4-bytes of memory, i.e., 2-bytes for segment address and 2-byte for offset address. Thus a far pointer is a 32-bit address. A far pointer can address any location within the 1 MB address space.

The programs using far pointers runs slower than the program using near pointers. But the use of far pointers permit you to address any location outside the currently loaded segment and allow you to have larger programs and data.

However, the far pointers suffer from the following problems.

- Most pointer comparisons will not generate correct results. The reason for this is that when far pointers are compared using logical operators == and !=, then the full 32-bit value is used. For other logical operations only offset value is used. As the various segments can overlap, the various combination of segment:offset may map to same physical address.
- Incrementing/decrementing a far pointer may cause a warp around. This is because, when a far pointer is incremented/ decremented, only offset address is incremented or decremented.

Let us consider the problem of comparisons among far pointers.

Consider the following declarations

```
char far *ptr_1 = 0x2200030;
char far *ptr_2 = 0x02220010;
```

which corresponds to segment:offset combinations 0220:0030 and 022:0010. Both ptr_1 and ptr_2 address same memory location whose physical address (20-bit address) is 02230.

- Comparison, ptr_1 == ptr_2, will fail because the 32-it values are different.

- Comparision, ptr_1 != ptr_2, will hold.
- Comparusons, ptr_1 > ptr_2 and ptr_1 >=ptr_2 will hold because the offset value of ptr_1 (0030) is greater than offset value of ptr_2 (0010).
- Comparisons, ptr_1 < ptr_2 and ptr_1 <= ptr_2, will fail because the offset value of ptr_1 (0030) is neither less than nor equal to the offset value of ptr_2 (0010).

Let us now turn to the problem of wrap around while incrementing/decrementing a far pointer. For example, if the value of far pointer to a character type is 0ABC:FFFF, incrementing it will yield 0ABC:0000, which is the address of the first location in the segment.

Similarly, if the value of far pointer to character type is 0aBC:0000, decrementing it will yield 0ABC:FFFF, which is the address of the last location in the segment.

Huge Pointers

Huge pointers are similar to far pointers, but do not suffer from limitations of far pointers. The huge pointers are always kept normalized. By normalisation means the maximum address is adjusted in the segment address.

Since each segment can start only from paragraph boundary, the offset address will always be from 0 to F. Now the question arises – how huge pointers are normalised? The procedure is described below.

The setment:offset address is converted to 20-bit physical address by address calculation scheme and then the left most 16-bits are assigned to segment and the rightmost 4-bits to offset. For example, suppose the address in segment:offset form is 0220:0030. After address, calculations we get 02230 as the actual address.

This can be rewritten as 0223:0000, which is a normalised address. Similarly, the address 0222:0010, after address calculation yield 02230 which are on normalization will give 0223:000.

The normalisation process ensures that there is only one segment:offset combination of the huge address. Thus, all comparisons will be valid. Similarly when ever a huge pointer is incremented/decremented past a segment boundary, the segment address is adjusted accordingly.

However, the normalisation process takes some time, thus slowing down the executing speed. Also, the arithmetic operations on huge pointers are performed by calling special routines. Because of this, arithmetic operation on huge pointer are significantly slower. So this is the price which have to be paid for using huge pointers.

Turbo C Memory Models

Turbo C for the 8086 family of processors can compile the program in a six different ways, called memory models. Each one organizes the memory in the computer differently and effects the various aspects of program's performance.

There are six memory models supported by Turbo C. There are

tiny	small	medium
compact	large and	huge model.

Let us see how these models differ.

Tiny Model

The tiny model compiles the program so that the code and data must be in the same segment. All addressing is done using near pointers. The size of the program can be maximum of 64KB. This method of compilation produces the smallest and fastest code.

Small Model

The small model, the default model, compiles the program so that the code is in one segment and data in another segment. All addressing is done using near pointers.

The execution speed of programs compiled is as good as of compiled in tiny model, but the programs can be approximately twice as big.

Medium Model

This model compiles the program so that the code can be in more tan one segment but data in one segment. The medium model is for large programs where the program size is more than 64KB, but the data requirements are less.

All addressing for the code is done using far pointers, where as addressing for data is done using near pointers. In these programs, the references to the functions will take more time, whereas the references to the data will take same time as in small model.

Compact Model

The compact model is complementary to the medium model. The

compact model compiles the program so that the code must be in one segment, but the data can be in more than one segment. he compact model is for programs where the program size is not more than 64KB but the data requirements are more.

All addressing for the code is done using near pointers, where as addressing for data is done using far pointers. in these programs the references to the functions will take same time as in small model, whereas the references to the data will take more time.

Large Model

The large model compiles the program so that both the code and the data can use multiple segments. The single item of data, such as an array is limited to 64K. The large model is for the programs where the program size is more than 64KB and the data requirements are also more. All addressing is done using far pointers.

Huge Model

The huge model is same as the large model except that the single item of data, such as an array, can exceed the limited of 64K. All addressing is done using huge pointers. Program compiled in this model runs slower than large model.

Memory Models (in segments)	*Code Size*	*Data Size*	*Code Pointer*	*Data Pointer*	*Program Speed*
Tiny	One	One	Near	Near	Fastest
Small	One	One	Near	Near	Fastest
Medium	More	One	Far	Near	Fastest
Compact	One	More	Near	Far	Fastest
Large	More	More	Far	Far	Fastest
Huge	More	More	Far	Huge	Slowest

Compiler Options for Memory Models

Turbo C compiles the program using small model, by default. To use different memory model you must tell the compiler. In the IDE, you can do this be using Compiler sub option under Options menu. For the command-line version, you can use one of the options.

Memory Model	*Option*
Tiny	-mt
Small(default)	-ms
Medium	-mm
Compact	-mc
Large	-ml
Huge	-mh

Overriding a Memory Model

Sometimes even a single reference to a data in another segment may force you to use a compact model rather than small model, thus degrading the execution speed of the entire program though only a few references are for another segment. In practice, this type of situation arises in different ways.

For example, your entire program might need only near pointers with few references to the video RAM of a PC. The video RAM is a part of memory dedicated to the display and needs far addressing. This problem can be handled by using a pointer modifiers – near, far, or huge.

When these modifiers are used, they effect the way data is accessed. It is also possible to use near and far modifiers for functions. In this case they effect the way in which the function call and return from the function is performed.

These modifiers follow the data type specifier and precede the variable name.

For example, the statement

```
char far *ptr;
```

declares a far pointer called ptr to character type.

Similarly, the following statement

```
void far sample(void);
```

declares a function named sample() of far type.

4 ARRAYS IN C

> An array can be found in most of the programming language. It is used to store same type of value in different variables.

Introduction

Each program stores information in variables. To store multiple values, the program uses a special data structure, called an Array. Simply speaking, an array is a variable that can hold multiple values of the same type, such as 10 values type int.

To declare an array, your programs must specify array type, name, and number of items the array will store.

Various features of an array are:

- An array is a data structure that lets a single variable store multiple values of the same type
- When you declare an array, you must specify the type of value the array will store as well as the number of items the array will hold.
- Each element within an array must be the same type, such as int, float, or char.
- To store a value within an array, you specify the element number within the array at which you want to store the value. For example, the array's first element is element 0, the second is element 1, and so on.
- To access a value stored within an array, your programs specify the array name and the element number, placing the element number within left and right brackets, such as scores{9}.
- When your program declares an array, it can use the assignment operator to initialise array elements.
- Your programs can pass array variables to functions just as they would any parameter.

Let us try to write a program to find average marks obtained by a class of 20 students in an exam.

```
/* Print exam marks
main()
{
   float avg, sum=0;
   int i;
   int marks[20]; /* array declaration*/
   for (i=0; i<=19; i++)
   {
      printf ("\nEnter marks");
      scanf ("%d", &marks[i]); /* store data in
               array */
   }
   for (i=0; i<=19; i++)
      sum = sum + marks[i]; /* read data from an
               array*/
   avg = sum / 20;
   printf ("\nAverage marks = %f", avg);
}
```

As you can see from the program we have defined an array, stored information in it and then retrieved it from the array.

Arrays are of different types:

one-dimensional arrays, comprised of finite homogeneous elements.

multi-dimensional arrays, comprised of elements, each of which is itself an array.

A two-dimensional array is the simplest of multidimensional arrays. However, C allows arrays of more than two dimensions.

Single Dimensional Arrays

The simplest form of an array is a single dimensional array. The array is given a name and its elements are referred to by their subscripts or indices. C array's index numbering starts with 0. An array definition specifies a variable type and a name along with one more feature size to specify how many data items the array will contain. The general form of an array declaration is as shown below:

```
type array-name [size] ;
```

where type declares the base type of the array, which is the type of each element in the array. The array-name specifies the name with which the array will be referenced and size defines how many elements the array will hold. The size must be an integer value or integer constant without any sign.

The data type of array elements is known as the base type of the array.

Following statement declares an array marks of base type int and which can hold 50 elements.

```
int marks [50] ;
```

The above statement declared array marks has 50 elements, marks [0] to marks [49]. A vector is a mathematical term, which refers to the collection of numbers which are analogous, i.e., a linear array (one dimensional arrays) and a vector in C can represent only integers and floating-point numbers.

String as an Array

C does not have a string data type rather it implements strings as single-dimension character arrays. A string is defined as a character array that is terminated by a null character '\0'. For this reason, the character arrays are declared one character longer than the largest string they can hold. For instance, to declare an array strg that holds a 10-character string, you would write

```
char strg[11];
```

This makes room for the null character at the end of the string.

Individual characters of a string can be easily accessed as they make the elements of the character array, The index 0 refers to the first character, the index 1 to the second 2 to the third, and so forth, The end of a string is determined by checking for null character.

Two-Dimensional Arrays

A two-dimensional array is an array in which each element is itself an array. For instance, an array A [M] [N] is an M by N table with M rows and N columns containing M x N elements. The number of elements in a 2-D array can be determined by multiplying number of rows with number of columns. For example, the number of elements in an array A [7] [9] is calculated as 7 x 9 = 63. The simplest form of a multidimensional array, the two-dimensional array, is an array having simple-dimension arrays as its elements.

The general form of a two-dimensional array declaration in C is as follows :

```
type array-name [rows] [columns];
```

where type is the base data type of the array having name array-name; rows, the first index, refers to the number of rows in the array and columns, the second index, refers to the number of columns in the array.

Following declaration declares an int array sales of size 5, 12.

```
Int sales[5][12];
```

The array sales have 5 elements sales [0], sales [1], sales [2], sales [3] and sales [4] each of which is itself an int array with 12 elements. The elements of sales are referred to as sales [0][0], sales [0][1], ... sales [0][11], sales [1][0], sales [1][1], and so forth.

Array of Strings

An array of strings is a two-dimensional character array. The size of first index (rows) determines the number of strings and the size of second index (columns) determines maximum length of each string. The following code declares an array of 10 strings, each of which can hold maximum 50 valid characters.

```
char strings[10][51];
```

Notice that the second index has been given value 51, i.e., 1 extra to take care of the null character '\0'.

It is very easy to access an individual string by just specifying the first index, an individual string can be accessed. For instance, from the array string[5][7] string[1] would give you "Second" ; string[4] would give you "Fifth".

Array Initialization

The general form of array initialization is as shown below:

```
type array-name [size N] = {value-list};
```

The value-list is a comma-separated list of array elements' values. The element values in the value-list must have the same data type as that of type, the base type of the array.

Following code initializes an integer array with 12 elements.

```
int days-of-month [12] = {31, 28, 31, 30, 31, 30, 31, 31, 30, 31, 30, 31} ;
```

This would place first value 31 in month [1], 28 in month [2], and so on.

Character arrays can also be initialized like this as shown below:

```
char string [10] = "Program" ;
```

The above code will initialize the string with "Program".

Alternatively, above declaration can be written as :

```
char string [10] =  {'P', 'r', 'o', 'g', 'r', 'a',
            'm', '\0'} ;
```

Because all strings in C terminate with a null, you must make sure that the array you declare is long enough to include the null.

Two-dimensional arrays are also initialized in the same way as single-dimension ones.

For example, the following code initializes a two-dimensional array cube with numbers 1 through 5 and their cubes:

```
int cube[5][2] =:  { 1 , 1,
   2, 8,
   3, 27,
   4, 64
   5 125}
```

Using Array

Let us try to write a program to find average marks obtained by a class of 30 students in a test.

```
main()
{
   float avg, sum = 0;
   int i;
   int marks[30]; /* array declaration */

   for (i = 0; i <=29;i++)
   {
      printf ("\nEnter marks");
      scanf  ("%d", &marks[i]; /* store data in
            array */
```

```
    }

    for (I = 0; <= 29;i++)
      sum = sum + marks[i[; /*read data from an
              array */

    avg = sum / 30
    printf ("\nAgerage marks = %f", avg);
}
```

Let us see what this program has to offer.

Declaring an Array

Like other variables an array has to be declared so that the compiler will know what kind of an array and how large an array you want. In the last program this was done this with the statement:

```
int marks[30];
```

Here, int specifies the type of the variable, just as it does with ordinary variables and the word marks specifies the name of the variable. The [30] however is new.

The number 30 tells how many elements of the type int will be in the array. This number is often called the 'dimension' of the array. The bracket ([ ]) tells the compiler that you are dealing with an array.

Accessing Array Elements

Once an array is declared, let us see how individual elements in the array can be referred. This is done with subscript, the number in the brackets following the array name. This number specifies the element's position in the array.

All the array elements are numbered, starting with 0. Thus, marks[2] is not the second element of the array but the third. In above program the variable i is used as a subscript to refer to various elements of the array. This variable can take different values and hence can refer to the different elements in the array in turn. This ability to use variables as subscripts is what makes arrays so useful.

Entering Data into an Array

Here is the section of code that places data into the array:

```
for (i = 0; i <=29;i++)
```

```
{
   printf ("\nEnter marks");
   scanf ("d", &marks[i]);
}
```

The for loop causes the process of asking for and receiving a student's marks from the user to be repeated 30 times. The first time through the loop, i has a value 0, so the scanf() statement will cause the value typed to be stored in the array element marks[0], the first element of the array.

This process will be repeated until i becomes 29. This is last time through the loop, which is a good thing, because there is no array element like marks[30].

In the scanf() statement, the "address of" operator (&) on the element marks[i] of the array is used, just as it was earlier used on other variables (&rate, for example). In doing so, you are passing the address of this particular array element of the scanf() function, rather than its value; which is what scanf() requires.

Reading Data from an Array

The balance of the program reads the data back out of the array and uses it to calculate the average. The for loop is much the same, but now the body of the loop causes each student's marks to be added to a running total stored in a variable called sum.

When all the marks have been added up, the result is divided by 30, the number of students, to get the average.

```
for (I = 0; I <=29; i++)
   sum = sum + marks[i];
avg = sum / 30 ;
printf ("\nAverage marks = %f", avg) ;
```

To fix our ideas, let us revise whatever we have learnt about arrays:

1. An array is a collection of similar elements.
2. The first element in the array is numbered 0, so the last element is 1 less tan the size of the array.
3. An array is also known as a subscripted variable.
4 Before using an array its type and dimension must be declared.
5. However bit an array its elements are always stored in contiguous memory locations. This will be discussed later.

Array Elements in Memory

Consider the following array declaration:

```
int arr[8];
```

What happens in memory when we make this declaration? 16 bytes get immediately reserved in memory. 16, because each of 8 integers would be 2 bytes long. And since the array is not being initialised, all eight values present in it would be garbage values.

This so happens because the storage class of this array is assumed to be auto. If the storage class is declared to the static then all the array elements would have a default initial value as zero. Whatever be the initial values all the array elements would always be present in contiguous memory locations.

Bounds checking

In C there is no check to see if the subscript used for an array exceeds the size of the array. Data entered with a subscript exceeding the array size will simply be placed in memory outside the array; probably on top of other data, or an the program itself.

This will lead to unpredictable results, to say the least and there will be no error message to warn you that you are going beyond the array size. In some cases the computer may just hang. Thus, the following program may turn out to be suicidal.

```
main()
{
    int num{40]. I;

    for (i = 0; I <= 100;i++)
        num[i] = I;
}
```

Thus, to see to it that we do not reach beyond the array size is entirely the programmer's botheration and not the compiler's.

Passing Elements to A Function

Array elements can be passed to a function by calling the function by value, or by reference. In the call by value we pass values of array elements to the function, whereas in the call by reference we pass addresses of array elements to the function.

These two calls are illustrated below:

```
/* Demonstration of call by value */
main()
{
   int i ;
   int marks [] = { 55, 65, 75, 78, 78, 90);

   for (i = 0; i <=6; i++)
      display (marks[i] ;
}
display (int m)
{
   printf ("%d", m);
}
```

And here's the output....

```
   55 65 75 78 78 90
```

Here, we are passing an individual array element at a time to the function display () and getting it printed in the function display (). Note that since at a time only one element is being passed, this element is collected in an ordinary integer variable m, in the function display ().

And now the call by reference.

```
/* Demonstration of call by reference */
main()
{
   int I;
   int marks[] = 55, 65, 75, 56, 78, 78, 90};

   for (i = 0; I <=6; i++)
      disp (&marks[i] );
}


disp (int *n)
{
```

```
    printf ("%d", *n);
}
```

And here's the output....

```
    55 65 75 56 78 78 90
```

Here, we are passing addresses of individual array elements to the function display(). Hence, the variable in which this address is collected (n) is declared as a pointer variable. And since n contains the address of array element, to print out the array element we are using the 'value at address' operator (*).

```
main()
{
    int i;
    int marks [] = {55, 65, 75, 56, 78, 78, 90};

    for (i = 0 ; I <=6; i++)
        disp (&marks[i]) ;
}
disp (int *n)
{
    show (&n);
}
```

Pointers and Arrays

To be able to see what pointers have got to do with arrays, let us first learn some pointer arithmetic. Consider the following example:

```
main()
{
    int I = 3, *x;
    float j = 1.5, *y;
    char k = 'c' *z;

    printf ("\nValue of i = %d", i) ;
    printf ("\nValue of j = %f", j) ;
```

```
    printf ("\nValue of k = %c", k)  ;
    x = &I;
    y = &j;
    z = &k;
    printf ("\nOriginal address in x = %u",x);
    printf ("\nOriginal address in y = %u",y);
    printf ("\nOriginal address in z = %u",z);
    x++;
    y++;
    z++;
    printf ("\nNew address in x = %u",x);
    printf ("\nNew address in y = %u",y);
    printf ("\nNew address in z = %u",z);
}
```

Suppose i, j and k are stored in memory at addresses 1002, 2004 and 5006 the output would be......

```
Value of i = 3
Value of j = 1.5
Value of k = c
Original address in x = 1002
Original address in y = 2004
Original address in x = 5006
New address in x = 1004
New address in y = 2008
New address in x = 5007
```

The way a pointer can be incremented, it can be decremented as well, to point to earlier locations. Thus, the following operations can be performed on a pointer:

1. Addition of a number to a pointer.

   For example,

```
int = 4, *j, *k;
j = &I;
j = j + 1;
```

```
j = j + 9;
k = j + 3;
```

2. Subtraction of a number from a pointer.

   For example,

```
int I = 4, *j, *k;
j = & I;
j = j - 2;
j = j - 5;
k = j - 6;
```

3. Subtraction of one pointer from another.

   One pointer variable can be subtracted from another provided both variables point to elements of the same array. The resulting value indicates the number of bytes of separating the corresponding array elements. This is illustrated in the following program.

```
main()
{
   int arr[] = {10, 20, 30, 45, 67, 56, 74};
   int *j, 8j;

   i = &arr[1];
   j = &arr[5];
   printf ("%d%d", j, -i, *j - *i);
}
```

Here i and j have been declared as integer pointers holding addresses of first and fifth element of the array respectively.

4. Comparison of two pointer variables

   Pointer variables can be compared provided both variables point to objects of the same data type. Such comparisons can be useful when both pointer variables point to elements of the same array. The comparison can test for either equality r inequality. Moreover, a pointer variable can be compared with zero (usually expressed as NULL). The following program illustrates how the comparison is carried out.

```
main()
```

```
{
    int arr [ ] = { 10, 20, 36, 72, 45, 36) ;
    int *j, *k ;

    j = &arr [ 4 ];
    k = (arr + 4 );

    if (j == k)
        printf ("The two pointers point to the
            same location");
    else
        printf ("The two pointers do not point to
            the same loction");
}
```

Remember! Do not attempt the following expirations on pointers ..... they would never work out.

1. Addition of two pointers
2. Multiplication of a pointer with a constant
3. Division of a pointer with a constant

Here is a program that prints out the memory locations in which the elements of this array are stored.

```
main()
{
    int num [ ] = 24, 34, 12, 44, 56, 17 } ;
    int I ;

    for ( I = 0; I <= 5; i++)
    {
        printf ("\nelement no. %d",i);
        printf (address = %u, &num[i] );
    }
}
```

The output of this program would look like this:

```
element no. 1 address = 4001
element no. 1 address = 4003
element no. 2 address = 4005
element no. 3 address = 4007
element no. 4 address = 4009
element no. 5 address = 4011
```

Note that the array elements are stored in contiguous memory locations, each element occupying two bytes, since it is an integer array.

When you run this program, you make get different addresses, but what is certain is that each subsequent address would be 2 bytes greater than its immediate predecessor.

The next two programs show ways in which you can access the elements of this array.

```
main()
{
    int num [ ] = {24, 34, 12, 44, 56, 17};
    int i;

    for (i = 0; i<=5; i++)
    {
        printf ("\naddress = %u", &num[i]);
        printf ("element = %d", num[i]);
    }
}
```

The output of this program would be:

```
address = 4001 element = 24
address = 4003 element = 34
address = 4005 element = 12
address = 4007 element = 44
address = 4009 element = 56
address = 4011 element = 17
```

The method of accessing array elements by using subscripted variables is already known to us.

This method has in fact been given here for easy comparison with the next method, which accesses the array elements using pointers.

```
main()
{
    int num [ ] = {24, 34, 12, 44, 56, 17};
    int i, *j;
    j=&num[0]; /*assign adress of zeroeth element*/

    for (i = 0; i<=5; i++)
    {
        printf ("\naddress = %u", &num[i]);
        printf ("element = %d", *j);
        j++; /*increment pointer to point to next
             location */
    }
}
```

The output of this program would be:

```
address = 4001 element = 24
address = 4003 element = 34
address = 4005 element = 12
address = 4007 element = 44
address = 4009 element = 56
address = 4011 element = 17
```

In this program, to begin with we have collected the base address of the array (address of the oth element) in the variable j using the statement,

```
j=&num[0]; /* assigns address 4001 to j */
```

When we are inside the loop for the first time, j contains the address 4001 and the value at this address is 24. These are printed using the statements,

```
printf ("\naddress = %u, j);
printf ("element = %d", *j);
```

On incrementing j it points to the next memory location of its type (that is location no. 4003). But location no. 4003 contains the second element of the array, therefore when the printf( ) statements are executed for the second time they print out the second element of the array and its address (i.e., 34 and 4003).. and so on till the last element of the array has been printed.

Obviously, a question arises as to which of the above two methods should be used when?

Accessing array elements by pointers is always faster than accessing them by subscripts.

However, from the point of view of convenience in programming we should observe the following:

— Array elements should be accessed using pointers if the elements are to be accessed in a fixed order, say from beginning to end, or from end to beginning, or every alternate element or any such definite logic.

— Instead, it would be easier to access the elements using a subscript if there is no fixed logic in accessing the elements. However, in this case also, accessing the elements by pointers would work faster than subscripts.

5 STRINGS IN C

Strings are commonly used to define a length of text namely, words and sentences.

Introduction

Strings are the way of manipulating text such as words and sentences. It is not that C controls only characters it can handle numeric too. A string constant is a one dimensional array of characters terminated by a null ('\0'). For example,

```
char name[] = {'S', 'A', 'C', 'H', 'I', 'N', '\0'}
```

The terminating null ('0') is important, because it is the only way the functions that work with a string can know where the string ends.

You can even use the string to initialization as shown below:

```
char name[] = "SACHIN";
```

Notice in this case the null character is not there. In this case C inserts a null character automatically.

Another example of the string is as follows:

```
/* Print your name from a string
main()
{
   char name(30);
   print ("\nEnter your name");
   scanf ("%a", name);
   printf ("Good Morning %a!", name);
}
```

This will have the following output

Enter your name   Ramesh

Good Morning Ramesh!

Well in this program I had reserved 30 characters for the name, you can set aside more characters if your name is long.

Please note that the length of the string should not exceed the dimension of the character array. This is because the C compiler does not perform bounds checking on character arrays.

Also you are not allowed to have multiple-word strings. For example you cannot have the name as Ramesh Bangia, compiler would not accept that. However, this you can overcome using the gets() function and its counterpart puts().

So now the program can be changed in the following manner.

```
/* Print your name from a string
main()
{
   char name(30);
   print ("\nEnter your name");
   gets (name);
   puts ("Good morning!")
   puts (name);
}
```

This would output like this:

Enter your name   Ramesh Bangia

Good Morning!

Ramesh Bangia

You must be wondering why I have not combined Good Morning with Ramesh Bangia. Well, wish I could do this. There is a limit of one string at a time in the function put().

Also it prints in the next line so you do not have to give the printf() function.

Library Strings

C compiler comes with a number of strings which are readily available for you to use.

Following is the list of these strings and their usage.

Function	Use
strcat	Appends one string to another
strchr	Finds first occurrence of a given character in a string

strcmp	Compares two strings
strcpy	Copies one string to another
strdup	Duplicates a string
stricmp	Compares two strings without regard to case
strlen	Finds length of a string
strlwr	Converts a string to lowercase
strncat	Appends a portion of one string to another
strncmp	Compares a portion of one string with portion of another string
strncpy	Copies a given number of characters of one string to another
strnicmp	Compares a portion of one string with a portion of another without regard to case
strrchr	Finds last occurrence of a given character in a string
strrev	Reverses a string
strset	Sets all characters in a string to a given character
strstr	Finds first occurrence of a given string in another string

Out of the above strings, let us look at 2 of them, i.e., strcpy() and strcmp().

strcpy()

As mentioned in the table above, this string is used to copy contents of one string into another. This can be illustrated with the help of the following example.

```
/* Use of the string strcpy
main()
{
   char source[] = "Sachin";
   char target[25];
   strcpy (target, source);
   printf ("\nsource string = %s", source);
   printf ("\ntarget string = %s", target);
}
```

This will result in the following output:

source sting = Sachin

target string = Sachin

strcmp()

As mentioned in the table above, this string is used to compare two strings to find out whether they are same or different.

If the two strings are identical, strcmp() returns a value zero. If they are not it returns the numeric difference between the ASCII value of the non-matching characters.

This can be illustrated with the help of the following example.

```
/* Use of the string strcmp
main()
{

    char string1[] = "Sachin";
    char string2[] = "Vachin"
    int i,j,k;
    i = strcmp (string1, "Sachin");
    j = strcmp (string2, string2);
    k = strcmp (string1, "Sachin boy");
    printf ("\n%d %d %d, i,j,k);
}
```

This will result in the following output:

3 -32

In the first case the difference between Sachin and Vachin is the presence of S and V. The ASCII value of S is 83 and that of V is 86, so the difference of 3 is reflected in output.

In the second case there is blank after Sachin which has resulted in -32 which is the ASCII value of a null character.

6 Input Output Operations in C

> Most of the inputs are through keyboards and the outputs are either on monitor or printers.

Introduction

C has no provisions for reading and writing the input and output. In fact there is no command for writing to the floppy or reading from it. On the other hand it has no provision for sending the data to the monitor for displaying the results. Only commands available with C are print() and scan().

Types of I/O

Each Operating System has it's own facility for inputting and outputting data from and to the files and devices. It's simple matter for a system programmer to write a few small programs that would link the C compiler for particular Operating system's I/O facilities. The developers of C Compilers do just that. They write several standard I/O functions and put them in libraries.

Though these functions are not part of C's formal definition, they have becme a standard feature of C language and hae been initiated more or less faithfully by every designer of a DOS based or a UNIX based C Compilers. Whatever version of C you are using it's almost certain that you have access to such a library of I/O functions.

In fact, the way DOS displays an output on screen is different than the way UNIX does it. Fortunately, the printf( ) function that we use on a DOS based C compiler works even with a UNIX based C compiler. This is because, the standard library function printf( ) for DOS based C compiler has been written keeping in mind the way DOS output characters to screen.

Similarly, the printf( ) function for a UNIX based compiler has been written keeping in mind the way UNIX outputs characters to screen. We, as users do not have to bother about which printf( ) has been written in what manner. We should just use printf( ) and it would take care of the rest of the details. Same is true about all other standard library functions available for I/O.

The various library functions available for input output in C can be classified into 3 broad categories:

Console I/O functions

These functions are there to receive input from keyboard and to write output to VDU.

Disk I/O functions

These functions are there to perform I/O operations on a floppy disk or hard disk.

Port I/O functions

These functions are there to perform I/O operation on various ports of the computer.

Let us now take a close look at each of these.

Console I/O functions

Console I/O functions can be further classified into two categories:

formatted and

unformatted console I/O functions.

The main difference between them is that the formatted functions allow the input read from the keyboard or the output displayed on the VDU to be formatted as per our requirements. For example, if values of average marks and percentage marks are to be displayed on the screen, then the details like where this output would appear on the screen, how many spaces would be present between the two values, the number of places after the decimal points, etc., can be controlled using formatted functions.

Formatted functions

Type	*Input*	*Output*
char	scanf()	printf()
int	scanf()	printf()
float	scanf()	printf()
string	scanf()	printf()

UnFormatted functions

Type	*Input*	*Output*
char	getch()	putch()
	getche()	putchar()
	getchar()	
int	—	—
float	—	—
string	gets()	puts()

Now let us discuss these console I/O functions in detail.

Formatted Console I/O Functions

The functions printf( ) and scanf( ) fall under the category for formatted console I/O functions. These functions allow us to supply the input in a fixed format and let us obtain the output in the specified form. Let us discuss these functions one by one. But, first of all let us understand printf( ) and its use in C. In its general form this command looks like this....

```
printf ("format string", list of variables);
```

The format string can contain:

- characters that are simply printed as t hey are
- conversion specifications that begin with a % sing
- escape sequences that begin with a \ sing

For example, look at the following program:

```
main()
{
   int avg = 643;
   float per = 39.6;
   printf ("Average=%d\nPercentage=%f", avg, per);
}
```

The output of the program would be.....

```
Average = 643

Percentage = 39.600000
```

How does printf() functions interpret the contents of the format string. For this it examines the format string form left to right. So long as it doesn't come across either a % or a \, it continues to dump the characters that it encounters, on to the screen.

In this example Average = is dumped on the screen. The moment it comes across a conversion specification in the format string, it picks up the first variable in the list of variables and prints its value in the specified format. In this example, the moment %d is met the variable avg is picked up and its value is printed.

Similarly, the moment an escape sequence is met it takes the appropriate action. Here, the moment \n is met it places the cursor at the beginning of the next line. This process continues till the end of format string is reached.

Conversion Specifications

The %d %f used in the printf() are called conversion characters. They tell /printf() to print the value of avg as a decimal integer and the value of per as a float. Following is the list of conversion characters that can be used used with the printf() functions.

Data type	*Conversion character*	
Integer	short signed	%d or %i
	short unsigned	%u
	long signed	%ld
	long unsigned	%lu
	unsigned hexadecimal	%x
	unsigned octal	%o
Real	float	%f
	double	%lf
character	signed character	%c
	unsigned character	%c
string		%s

We can provide following optional specifiers in the conversion specifications.

Specifier	*Description*
dd	digits specifying field width

	decimal point separating field width from precision (precision stands for the number of places after the decimal point)
dd	digits specifying precision
–	minus sign for left justifying the output in the specified field width

The field width specifier tells printf() how many columns on screen should be used while printing a value. The following example would make it more clear.

```
main()
{
   int weight = 36;

   printf ("\nweight is %d kg", weight);
   printf ("\nweight is %2d kg", weight);
   printf ("\nweight is %4d kg", weight);
   printf ("\nweight is %6d kg", weight);
   printf ("\nweight is %-6d kg", weight);
}
```

The output of the program would look like this.......

```
columns  0123456789012345678901234567890
         weight    is 36 kg
         weght     is 36 kg
         weight    is   36 kg
         weight    is     36 kg
         weight    is 36     kg
```

Escape Sequences

In the last example, we had seen that \n creates a new line, when inserted in a printf()'s format string. It is called the newline character. The newline character is an 'escape sequence', so called because the backslash symbol (\) is considered an 'escape' character characters. It causes an escape from the normal interpretation of a string, so that the next character is recognised as one having a special meaning. This is demonstrated in the following example.

```
main()
{
   printf ("You\are\definitely\going\to\like\it");
}
```

the output would look like.

01234567890123456789012345678901234567890

You   are definitely   going

to   likeit

The cursor jumps over eight columns when it encounters the "\t" character. This is another useful technique for lining up columns of output. Most compilers allow the user to change the number of print zones available on the screen, thereby changing the tab width.

The following escape characters are in use.

Escape Characters

Esc. Seq.	*Purpose*
\n	New line
\b	Backspace
\f	Form feed
\'	Single quote
\\	Backslash
\t	Tab
\r	Carriage return
\a	Alert
\"	Double quote

You can use these escape characters whenever needed.

Scanf()

Let us now leave print() and see how scanf() is used. It allows us to enter data from keyboard that will be formatted in a certain way.

The general form of scanf() statement is as follows:

```
   scanf ("format string", list of addresses of
         variables);
```

For example:

```
scanf ("%d %f %c", &c, &a, &ch);
```

Note that we are sending addresses of variables (addresses are obtained by using '&' the 'address of' operator) to scanf() function. This is necessary because the values received form keyboard must be dropped into variables corresponding to these addresses. The values that are supplied through the keyboard must be separated by either blank(s), tab(s) or newsline(s). Do not include these escape sequences in the format string.

All the format specifications that we learnt in printf() function apply for scanf() function as well.

sprintf() and sscanf() Functions

The sprintf() function works similar to the printf() function except for one small difference. Instead of sending the output to the screen as printf() does, this function writes the output to an array of characters.

The following program illustrates this.

```
main()
(
    int i = 10;
    char ch = `A'
    float a = 3.14
    char str[20]
       printf("\n%d %c %f", i, ch, a);
       sprintf(str, "%d %c %f", i, ch, a);
       printf("\n%s", str);
}
```

Here the values of I, cha and a and printed on the screen. Also sprintf() stores these values in the character array str. Since the string str is present in memory what is written into str using sprintf() doesn't get displayed on the screen. After str has been built, its contents can be displayed on the screen. The second printf() statement does this.

Then there is a function called sscanf(), which is counterpart of sprinttf(). It allows us to read characters from a string and to convert and store them in C variables according to specified formats. The sscanf() function comes in handy for in-memory conversion of characters to values.

You may find it convenient to read in strings from a file and then extract values from a string by using sscanf(). The usage of sscanf() is same as scanf(), except that the first argument is the string from which reading is to take place.

Unformatted Console I/O Functions

In this category you will find the various standard library functions. A complete list of these functions are given in a later chapter. So far for input we have consistently used the scanf() function. However, for some situations the scanf() function has a drawback. You have to hit the Enter key before the function can accept what you have typed.

On the other hand, we often want a function that will read a single character the instant it is typed without waiting for the Enter key to be hit. getch() and gerche() are two such functions which serve this purpose. These functions return the character that has been most recently typed. The 'e' in getche() function means it displays the character that you typed on the screen.

As against this getch() just returns the character that you typed without displaying it on the screen. getchar() works similarly and displays the character that you typed on the screen, but unfortunately requires Enter key to be typed following the character that you typed. The difference between getchar() and fgetchar () is that the former is a macro whereas the letter is a function.

Here is a sample program which illustrates the use of these functions.

```
main()
{
   char ch;

   print ("\nPress any key to continue");
   getch() ; /* will not echo the character */

   printf ("\nType any character") ;
   ch = getche() ; /* will echo the character
              typed */

   printf ("\nType any character") ;
   gechar() ; /* will echo character, must be
              followed by enter key */
   printf ("\nContinue Y/N") ;
```

```
fgetchar() ; /* will echo character, must be
        followed by enter key */
}
```

And here is a sample run of this program....

```
Press any key to continue

Type any character B

Type any character W

Continue Y/N Y
```

putch() and putchar() on the other hand print a character on the screen. Thought the working of putch(), putchar() and fputchar() is concerned, it is exactly the same.

The following program illustrates this.

```
main()
{
   char ch = 'R';

   putch (ch);
   putchar (ch);
   fputchar (ch);
   putch ('B');
   putchar ('B');
   fputchar ('B');
}
```

This will give the output as:

```
RRRBBB
```

All of these putch( ), putchar( ) and fputchar( ) output only one character at a time.

gets( ) and puts( )

In C gets() is used to receive a string of data from the keyboard. Well scanf() function can be used for the same, but it has its own limitations, as shown in the following program.

```
main()
{
   char name[40] ;

   printf ("\nEnter name") ;
   scanf ("%s, name) ;
   printf ("%s, name) ;
}
```

And here is the output

Enter name Ramesh Bangia

Ramesh

It is now be understood that Bangia was never stored in array name[], because after Ramesh you had given a space. The momemnt this space is given C assumes that the word has been completed. So you get only half the result of what was expected.

Now you understand why scanf() is not used to get the data. The solution to this problem is to use gets( ) function. It is terminated when a Enter key is hit. Thus, spaces and tabs are perfectly acceptable as part of the input string.

Moreover, gets( ) gets a newline (\n) terminated string of characters from the keyboard and replaces the \n and a \0. The puts( ) function works exactly opposite to gets( ) function. It outputs a string to the screen.

Let us understand this by means of a program.

```
main()
{
   char  cricketer[40];
   puts ("Enter name") ;
   gets (cricketer) ; /*sends base address of
               array */
   puts ("Happy cricketing!") ;
   puts (cricketer) ;
}
```

Following is the sample output:

Enter name

```
Sachin Tendulkar

Happy cricketing!

Sachin Tendulkar
```

Did you notice anything here. The puts() function has been used twice, once for the name and then for Happy cricketing!. This is so because puts() can output only one string at a time. If we attempt to print two strings using puts( ), only the first one gets printed. Similarly unlike scanf( ), gets( ) can be used to read only one string at a time.

Disk Functions

Disk operations are performed on entities called files. There are a large number of standard library functions available for performing Disk or file Input/Output. These functions can be broadly divided into two categories:

(a) High level file I/O functions (also called standard I/O or stream I/O functions)

(b) Low level file I/O functions (also called system I/O functions)

High level Disk I/O functions are more commonly used in C programs, since they are easier to use than low level disk I/O functions. There is one basic difference between high level and low level disk I/O functions. High level disk I/O functions do their own buffer management, whereas in low level disk I/O functions, buffer management has to be done explicitly by the programmer.

Opening A File

For all the file operations, like reading and writing, you have to open the file. Opening a file establishes a link between the program and the operating system, about, which file we are going to access and how. We provide the operating system with the name of the file and whether we plan to read or write to it.

The link between our program and the operating system is a structure called FILE which has been defined in the header file "stdio.h" (standing for standard input/output header file). Therefore, it is necessary to always include this file when we are doing high level disk I/O. When we request the operating system to open a file, what we get back (fi the request is indeed granted), is a pointer to the structure FILE. That is why, we make the following declaration before opening the file.

```
FILE *fp;
```

For each file which is opened there is a FILE structure, which contains information about the file being used, such as its current size, its location in memory, etc.

More importantly it contains a character pointer which points to the character that is about to get read.

To understand this, look at the followng statements,

```
FILE *fp ;

fp = fopen ("RB1.C", "r") ;
```

where,

fp — It is a pointer variable, which contains address of the structure FILE which has been defined in the header file "stdio,h".

fopen( ) — It will open a file "RB1.C" in 'read' mode, which tells the C compiler that we would be reading the contents of the file. Note that "r" is a string and not a character; hence the double quotes and not single quotes. In fact, fopen( ) performs 3 important taks when you open the file in "r" mode:

(a) Firstly it searches on the disk the file to be opened.

(b) If the file is present, it loads the file from the disk into memory. Of course if the file is very big, then it loads the file part by part.

If the file is absent, fopen( ) returns a NULL. NULL is a macro defined in "stdio.h" which indicates that you failed to open the file.

(c) It sets up a character pointer (which is part of the FILE structure) which points to the first character of the chunk of memory where the file has been loaded.

File Opening Modes

We had earlier used read ("r") mode. However, "r" is but one of the several modes in which we can open a file. Following is a list of all possible modes in which a file can be opened. The tasks performed by fopen() when a file is opened in each of these modes are also mentioned.

"r" Searches file. If the file exists, loads it into memory and sets up a pointer which points to the first character in it. If the file doesn't exist it returns NULL.

Operations possible – reading from the file.

"w" Searches file. If the file exists, its contents are overwritten. If the file doesn't exist, a new file is created. Returns NULL, if unable to open file.

Operations possible – writing to the file.

"a" Searches file. If the first exists, loads in to memory and sets up a pointer which points to the first character in it. If the file doesn't exist, a new file created. Returns NULL, if unable to open file.

Operation possible – appending new contents at the end of file.

"r+" Searches file. If it exists, loads it into memory and sets up a pointer which points to the first character in it. If file doesn't exist it returns NULL.

Operations possible – reading existing contents, writing new contents, modifying existing contents of the file.

"w+" Searches file. If the file exists, its contents are destroyed. If the file doesn't exist a new file is created. returns Null, if unable to open file.

Operations possible – writing new contents, reading from back and modifying existing contents of the file.

"a+" Searches file. If the file exists, loads it into memory and sets up a pointer which points to the first character in it. If the file doesn't exist, a new file is created. Returns NULL, if unable to open file.

Operations possible – reading existing contents, appending new contents to end of file. Cannot modify existing contents.

Reading from a File

When you open the file its contents are brought into memory (partly or wholly) and a pointer points to the very first character. To read the file's contents from memory there exists a function called fgetc( ). This has been used in our sample program through,

```
ch = fgetc ( fp ) ;
```

fgetc( ) reads the character from current pointer position, advances the pointer position so that it now points to the next character and returns the character that is read, which we collected in the variable ch.

Note that once the file has been opened, we no longer refer to the file by its name, but through the file pointer fp.

Closing The File

When we have finished reading from the file, we need to close it. This is done using the function flcose() through the statement,

```
fclose( fp ) ;
```

This deactivates the file an hence it can no longer be accessed using getc(). Once again we don't use the filename but the file pointer fp.

Writing to A File

For this we use the function called fputc. The fputc() function is similar to the putch() function, in the sense that both output characters. However, putch() function always writes to the VDU, whereas, fputc() writes to the file.

The writing process continues till all characters from the source file have been written to the target file, following which the while loop terminates.

fclose() function

When you send a character off to a file by using fputc(), the character is actually stored in a buffer – an area in memory, rather than being immediately written to the disk. When the buffer is full, its contents are written to the disk at once.

Or if the program knows that the last character to be written to the disk has been received in the buffer, but it is still not full, it forces the buffer to be written to the disk by 'closing' the file. Another purpose that fclose() servers is, it frees the link used by the particular file and the associated buffers, so that these are available for other files.

7 LIBRARY FUNCTIONS IN C

As there are books in the library, there are functions in the C library and can be used whenever required.

Introduction

Every compiler of C comes with its own set of library functions. Following are the functions which you will find in some compiler or the other.

Mathematical Functions

abs

```
int abs(int x);
```

Returns absolute value of a integer number x.

fabs

```
double fabs(double x);
```

Returns absolute value of a real number x.

labs

```
long labs(long x);
```

Returns absolute value of a long integer number x.

fmod

```
doble fmod(double x, double y);
```

Returns x module y, the remainder of x/y.

cos

```
double cos(double x);
```

Returns the cosine of x, where is angle x is in radians.

acos

```
double acos(double x);
```

Returns cosine inverse of x.

cosh

```
double cosh(double x);
```

Returns hyperbolic cosine of x.

sin

```
double sin(double x);
```

Returns the sine of x, where is angle of x is in radians.

asin

```
double asin(double x);
```

Returns sine inverse of x.

sinh

```
double sinh(double x);
```

Returns hyperbolic sine of x.

tan

```
double tan(double x);
```

Returns the tangent of x, where angle x is in radians.

atan

```
double atan(double x);
```

Returns tangent inverse of x.

tanh

```
double tanh(double x);
```

Returns hyperbolic tangent of x.

String Functions

strncat

```
void *strncat(char *dest, const char *src, size_t
        maxlen);
```

Appends at most maxlen characters of src to dest.

strncpy

```
void *strcpy(char *dest, const char *src, size_t
        maxlen);
```

Copies at most maxlen characters of src to dest.

strncmp

```
int strncmp(const char *dest, const char *src,
        size_t maxlen);
```

Compares at most first maxlen characters of src and dest.

stricmp

```
int stricmp(const char *dest, const char *src);
```

Compares two strings src and dest without regard to case.

strnicmp

```
int strnicmp(const char *dest, const char *src,
        size_t maxlen);
```

Compares at most first maxlen characters of src and dest without regard to case.

strlwr

```
char *strlwr(char *s);
```

Converts a string to lowercase.

strupr

```
char *strupr(char *s);
```

Converts a string to uppercase.

strset

```
char *strset(char *s, int c);
```

Sets all characters of s to c.

strnset

```
char *strnset(char *s, int c, size_t n);
```

Sets first n characters of s to c.

strstr

```
char *strstr(const char *s1, const char *s2);
```

Finds the occurrence substring s1 in s2.

strchr

```
char *strchr(const char *s, int c);
```

Returns a pointer to the first occurrence of c in s.

strrchr

```
char *strrchr(const char *s, int c);
```

Returns a pointer to the first occurrence of c in s.

Character Classification Macros

toupper(c)

Converts character c to uppercase, if it is in lowercase otherwise no effect.

tolower(c)

Converts character c to lowercase, if it is in lowercase otherwise no effect.

toascii(c)

Converts c greater than 127 to the range 0-127 by clearing all but lower 7 bits.

islower(c)

True if c is a lowercase letter.

isupper(c)

True if c is a uppercase letter.

ispunct(c)

Tue if c is a punctuation character.

isspace(c)

True if c a is a space, tab, carriage return, newline, vertical tab, or formfeed.

isxdigit(c)

True if c is a hexadecimal digit.

isalnum(c)

True if c is a letter or digit.

isalpha(c)

True if c is a letter.

isdigit(c)

True if c is a digit.

iscntrl(c)

True if c is a delete character or ordinary control character.

isprint(c)

True if c is a printable character.

isgraph(c)

Like isprint except that the space character is excluded.

File Handling Functions

rename

```
int rename(const char *oldname, const char
        *newname);
```

Renames a file. On sucessfully renaming a file, it returns 0. On error it returns –1.

unlink

```
int unlink(const char *filename);
```

Deletes a file. If the file has read only attribute, it fails. Returns 0 on success and –1 on failure.

Directory Control Functions

chdir

```
int chdir(const char *path);
```

Changes current directory. Returns 0 on success and –1 on failure.

mkdir

```
int mkdir(const char *path);
```

Changes new directory. Returns 0 on success and –1 on failure.

rmdir

```
int rmdir(const char *path);
```

Changes existing directory. Returns 0 on success and –1 on failure.

getcwd

```
char *getcwd(char *buf, int buflen);
```

Gets current working directory. It returns a pointer to buffer. On error it returns NULL.

getcurdir

```
int getcurdir(int drive, char *directory);
```

Gets current directory for specified drive. Drive 0 is default, 1 for A, 2 for B, and so on.

getdisk

```
int getdisk(void);
```

Returns current drive number.

fnsplit

```
int fnsplit(const char *path, const char *drive,
        char *dir, char *name, char *exit);
```

Splits a path name into its component parts.

fnmerge

```
int fnmerge(const char *path, const char *drive,
        const char *dir, const char *name, const
        char *exit);
```

Builds a path from its component parts.

disable

```
void disable(void);
```

Disables all hardware interrupts except NULL.

enable

```
void enable(void);
```

Enables hardware interrupts.

Macros

FP_OFF

```
off_add = FP_OFF(farptr);
```

Returns offset address of a far pointer.

FP_SEG

```
seg_add = FP_OFF(farptr);
```

Points segment address of a far pointer.

MK_FP

```
farptr = MK_FP(seg_add, off_add);
```

Returns a far pointer made from segment address and offset address.

Graphics Functions

initgraph

```
void far initgraph(int far *graphdriver, int
        far *graphmode, char far *pathtodriver);
```

Initializes the graphics system.

closegraph

```
void far closegraph(void);
```

Shuts down the graphics system.

putpixel

```
void far putpixel(int x, int y, int color);
```

Plots pixel with specified color at point (x, y).

line

```
void far line(int x1, int y1, int x2, int y2);
```

Draws line from (x1, y1) to (x2, y2) using current color, line style and thickness.

moveto

```
void far moveto(int x, int y);
```

Changes current position to point (x, y).

lineto

```
void far lineto(int x, inty);
```

Draws line from current position to point (x, y).

circle

```
void far circle(int x, int y, int r);
```

Draws a circle of radius r centered at point (x, y).

cleardevice

```
void far cleardevice(void);
```

Clears the graphics screen.

bar

```
void far bar(int left, int top, int right, int
        bottom);
```

Draws a bar with left top corner at point (left, top) and right bottom corner at (right, bottom).

bar3d

```
void far bard(int left, int top, int right, int
        bottom, int depth, int topflag);
```

Draws a 3D bar with left top corner at point (left, top) and right bottom corner at (right, bottom) with depth depth.

arc

```
void far arc(int x, int y, int stangle, int
        endangle, int r);
```

Draws an arc of radius r centered at point (x, y) with starting angle stangle and ending angle endangle.

pieslice

```
void far pieslice(int x, int y, int stangle,
         int endangle, int r);
```

Draws and fills an pie slice of radius r centered at point (x, y) with starting angle stangle and ending angle endangle.

setviewport

```
unsigned far setviewport(int left, int top,
         int right, int bottom, int clip);
```

Sets the current viewport for graphics output. The default viewport is entire screen, set up during the installation of graphics system.

clearviewport

```
unsigned far clearviewport(void);
```

Clears the current viewport.

setcolor

```
void far setcolor(int color);
```

Sets the new drawing color.

setbkcolor

```
void far setbkcolor(int color);
```

sets the new background color.

imagesize

```
unsigned far imagesize(int left, int top, int
         right, int bottom);
```

Returns the number of bytes required in store a bit image. If the required size is ≥ 64KB, it returns 0xFFFF.

getimage

```
void far getimage(int left, int top, int right,
         int bottom, void far *bitmap);
```

Saves a bit image enclosed in region specified by point (left, top) as left-top corner point and (right, bottom) as right bottom corner point to a memory block pointed to by bitmap.

putimage

```
vod far putimage(int left, int top, void far
        *bitmap, int op);
```

Outputs a bit image created with getimage to the screen region with respect to left-top corner specified by point (left, top). The op value specifies how the image is to be combined with the existing screen contents.

floodfill

```
void far floodfill(int x, int y, int border);
```

Fills a bounded region, where point (x, y) is any point in that region, and border specifies the border color.

Time and Date Related Functions

clock

```
clock_t clock(void);
```

Returns the processor time used since the beginning of program execution measured in clock ticks.

ftime

```
void ftime(struct timeb *buf);
```

Gets and stores the current time in timeb structure.

difftime

```
double difftime(time_t time2, time_t time1);
```

Returns the difference between two times.

time

```
time_t time(time_t *timer);
```

Returns the current time elapsed since 00:00:00 GMT, January 1970, and stores the value in location pointed to by time.

settime

```
void settime(struct time_t *timep);
```

Sets MS-DOS system time specified in a structure pointed to by timep.

gettime

```
void gettime(struct time_t *timep);
```

Gets MS-DOS system time and stored in a structure pointed to by timep.

setdate

```
void setdate(struct time_t *timep);
```

Sets MS-DOS system date specified in a structure pointed to the datep.

getdate

```
void setdate(struct time_t *datep);
```

Gets MS-DOS system date and stores in a structure pointed to by datep.

Miscellaneous Functions

exit

```
void exit(int status);
```

Terminates program. Before terminating, buffered output is flushed, files are closed and _exit() function is called.

_exit

```
void _exit(int status);
```

Terminates program.

sleep

```
void sleep(unsigned seconds);
```

Suspend execution for given internal in seconds.

delay

```
void delay(unsigned millisecond);
```

Suspend execution for given internal in seconds.

sound

```
void sound(unsigned frequency);
```

Turns PC speaker on for given frequency in hzs.

nosound

```
void nosound(void);
```

Turns PC speaker off.

flush

```
int fflush(FILE *fp);
```

Flushes a stream.

kbhit

```
int kbhit(void);
```

Checks for recent keystrokes. If a keystroke is available, it returns non-zero value else zero value.

system

```
int system(const char *command);
```

Issues MS-DOS internal command or executes a .COM, a .EXE or a .BAT file.

abort

```
void abort(void);
```

Abnormally terminates a process.

8 UNIONS, STACKS, LINKS AND QUEUES

These are advanced topics of C and can be studied in details in an advanced book.

Introduction

Every book on C, discusses unions along with structures. This is because of the closeness of their characteristics. Like structures, unions are a collection of different types of objects but they need not be related to each other. Here lies the major difference. Members of a structure are logically related and that of a union is not a compulsion.

The following gives the prototype of unions:

```
union <union_name>
{
<type> member1;
<type> member2;
.
.
<type> membern;
} ;
```

A noteworthy point about unions is that when one member of the union is accessed, it is recommended that the other members are not used. This is because all the members of the union share the same memory space. So accessing different members of union at the same time would not result in the desired output.

Size of a structure is the sum of sizes of all its members including the 'padding' done by the compiler. But the size of the union is the largest size occupied by anyone of its data members. For example,

```
union employee{
int emp_id;
char sex;
} ;
```

Here the size of the union employee is only 2 as int is the largest memory occupying data type which is assumed to be 2 bytes in this book. Here, when emp_id is accessed, accessing sex would not give desired results.

Declaration of Union

Union structure or skeleton can be declared as given in the above section. The union variables can be declared in two ways. They are:

```
union employee {
int emp_id;
int mgr_id;
}empl;
union employee emp2;
```

Here empl and emp2 are of type union employee. Their data members can be accessed similarly to that of structures. Consider the following example,

```
empl.emp_id = 10;
```

Now, both emp_id and mgr_id have same memory address. So on accessing empl.mgr_id also gives the value 10.

Apart from this, unions can occur in structures and arrays and unions can contain arrays or structures as its data members. Initialization of union can be done only on its first data member. Thus for an union given below,

```
union try
{ int a;
float b;
};
```

can be initialized only with int as

```
union try try1 = {10}
will initialize try1 .a to 10.
```

Uses of Unions

- The major use of unions is memory space utilization. When a programmer is sure of two or more independent variables; and when one variable occurs the other variables will not be used – instead of allocating different memory spaces to all those variables, the best programming practice would be to define them in a union. Apart from this, there is no basic importance of unions being used in any other context.

enum Data Types

To just recap it, enum is user-defined unique type containing a range of named constants called enumerators.

Example;

```
enum days{mon=1/tues,wed,thur,fri,sat,sun};
```

Here, man refers to 1, tues refers to 2 and so on till sun refers to 7.

If initialization of elements is not given, it starts from 0 and the next element takes a constant value, one more than the previous element.

typedef Keyword

typedef in C provides the programmer the facility of creating new data type names. Prototype for typedef is:

```
typedef < data type > < name >
```

Example: typedef int integer

Here, every occurrence of integer is considered as int. That is, int gets a new name as integer.

Consider the following example:

```
typedef char* string;
string a, b;
/* a, b both are of type char* */
```

It should be noted that typedef does not create a new type, but merely gives existing types a new name. typedef is considered as one of the storage class. They can also be used to name complex structures. For example;

```
struct btree{
   int a;
   btree *left, *right;
   };
   typedef strut btree breenode;
```

Here, btreenode is another name given for struct btree. typedef is generally used for portability issues. It is easy to make changes when typedef is used with programs that have to be moved from one implementation to another.

Changing in one place reflects throughout the program. typedef also provides a proper way of documentation, increasing the readability of the program.

Example Algorithms

Data structures are the manner in which a set of data values are stored and retrieved. These storage and retrieval techniques put together are called as data structures. There are various kinds of data structures available. Discussing all these data structures, does not come under the scope of this book. We will discuss very important and primarily used data structures like

1. Stacks
2. Queue

In this section, we will also be discussing about the algorithms involved to create a linked list, insert elements into it, delete elements from it and perform search operations on it.

Stacks

Stack is a 'Last-In, First-Out' (LIFO) data structure. The data element pushed recently will be the data element retrieved in the pop operation. There are three basic operations that can be performed on a stack.

1. Push – Insert an element to the top of the stack
2. Pop – Removes an element from the top of the stack
3. Peek – Retrieve the value of the element at the top of the stack

A stack pointer 'top' needs to be maintained, so that the programmer knows where to push in or pop out an element. Example 5.8 illustrates the implementation of a stack.

Implementation of stack

```
/*********************************************
/* Program to implement a stack */
/*********************************************
#include <stdio.h>
# define MAXSIZE 20
/* maximum size of stack
void push(int);
int pop();
int peek();
void print();
int stack[MAXSIZE];
int top = 0;
int main (void)
{
  push ( 30 ) ;
  print ( ) ;
```

```
    /* prints: 30 */

    push(20) ;
    print ( ) ;
    /* prints: 30 20   */

    pop() ;
    print();
    /* prints: 30

    push(10);
    print() ;
    /* prints: 3010 */

    pop() ;
    print ( ) ;
    /* prints: 30 */
}
void push(int a)
/* Function to push an element into the stack * /
{
    if(top==MAXSIZE)/*Stack overflow condition*
    printf(<<Stack is full>>);
    else
    {
        stack[top] = a;
        top = top + 1;
    }
}
int pop()
/* Function to retrieve an element from the stack
        */
{
    if (top == 0) /* Stack underflow condition *
    printf ( <<Stack is empty>> ) ;
    else
    {
        top =top -1;
```

```
        return stack[top)
    }
}

int peek()
/*Function which gets the value from the top */
/*of the stack  */
{
    return stack[top-1];
}
void print()
/* Function to print the content of the stack */
{
    int i;
    for(i = 0; i <top; i++)
    printf("%d  ",stack[I]);
    printf (<<\n>>) ;
}
```

Queues

A Queue data structure can be compared to the long queues that we encounter in our common life. The first person in the queue would have remained in the queue for the longest time. Hence, queue is a FIFO (First-In, First-Out) data structure: The element that is stored in the queue for the longest time will be the one to be dequeued.

The entry point of the queue is called the rear end of the queue. The exit point of the queue is called the front end of the queue. The following basic operations are performed on a queue.

1. Enqueue (element)
2. Dequeue( )

The following example illustrates an implementation of an integer queue.

```
/.********************************************** /
/* Program to Implement a queue * /
/********************************************** /
#include <stdio.h>
# define QSIZE 5
```

```
/* maximum size of queue
int Queue[QSIZE]
int front == 0;
int rear = 0;
void Enqueue(int a)
int Dequeue();
void print();
int main(void)
{
   Enqueue(10)
   print();
   /* prints : 10  */

   Enqueue(20)
   print();
   /* prints: 10 20 30       */

   Enqueue(30)
   print();
   /* prints: 10 20 30  25*/

   Enqueue(15)
   print();
   /* prints: 10 20 30 25 15      */

   Dequeue();
   print();
   /* prints: 20 30 25 15  */

   Dequeue()
   print();
   /* prints 30 25 15 */
}
void Enqueueint (int a)
/* Function to insert element into the element
            into the que    */
{
   if (rear == QSIZE   /*Queue full condition */
```

```
   printf (<<Queue is full>>);
   else
   {
      Queue[rear] = a;
      rear = rear + 1;
   }
}
int Dequeue()
/* Function to retrieve element from the queue */
{
   if (front == rear) /* Queue empty condition * /
   printf ( "Queue is empty" ) ;
   else
   {
      front =front + 1;
      return Queue[front -1]  ;
   }
}
void print()
/* Function to print the contents of the queue* /
{
   int i;
   for(i = front; i<rear; i++ )
   printf("%d  ",Queue[i]);
   printf ( "\n" ) ;
}
```

Linked List Data Structure

Linked list are dynamic data structures, which can be used with a data collection that grows or shrinks during program execution. Data structures like stacks and queues discussed previously would be more useful when they can accommodate variable amount of data. Linked list could come handy in such situations. Linked list is basically a set of nodes, not necessarily in sequential order containing links to the next node. There are many kinds of linked list like singly linked list, doubly linked list and circularly linked list. In this section, we restrict our discussion with singly linked list.

Initializing a linked list

To create a linked list, first we have to design the node based on the data to be stored in the linked list. The following code creates a linked list to store integer data types. It is recommended to have the last next pointer initialized to NULL. A head node is created to keep track of the list. The first node of the linked list is generally called head node and operations like insert and delete concerning the head node should be avoided else the track of the linked list would be lost. Here, the element stored in the head node of the list is 0.

Initializing a linked list

```
# include <stdio.h>
# define MAX 20
# define BEG -1
# define END -2
typedef struct node node
void initializelist();
int insert(int, int);
int delete(int);
node* search(int);
void display();
struct node
{
  int n;
  node *next;
}*top=NULL;
/* structure of the node is given above /*
/* and the top */
/* pointer is initialized to NULL */

void initializelist()
{
  if((top=(node*)malloc(sizeof(node))) ::= NULL)
/*top is allocated memory to the sizeof */
/* the structure */
  {
    printf( Error in initializing list\n");
  exit(1);
  }
```

```
top -> n = 0;
top->next = NULL;
/* the element stored in top is zero and its */
/*link is NULL*/
}
void display()
{
   node *tmp;
tmp = top->next;
   while (tmp != NULL)
/* loop to display the contents of the linked */
/* list */
   {
      printf ( "'%d\n", tmp->n) ;
      tmp = tmp->next;
/* traversing through the list using tmp */
   }
}
```

Insertion and Deletion into a linked list

To insert an element in a linked list, we have to create a new node, store the value in the node and set it to the next pointer of the previous node. If the user wants to insert in a particular position then first the node has to be searched for, after which the node can be inserted. Consider the following example for a better understanding.

The following code gives the functions to insert and delete elements in a linked list.

Inserting and deleting in a linked list

```
int insert( int num, int pos)
{
   node *temp,*t;
   temp = (node*)malloc(sizeof(node));
   t = top;
   temp->n = num;
   temp->next = NULL;
/* creating a node to accommodate the given */
/* data */
   if ( pos == BEG )
```

```
/* code to insert the node at the beginning of */
/* the list */
   {
      temp->next = top->next;
      top->next = temp;
   }
   else if (pos == END)
/* code to insert the node at the end of */
/* the list
   {
      while (t->next ! = NULL)
         t = t->next;
      t->next = temp;
   }
   else
/* code to insert the node at the required */
/* position */
{
   t = search(pos);
   temp->next = t->next;
   t->next = temp;
}
}
int delete (int num)
{
   node *t, *prev;
   t = top;
   prev = top;
   while (t !=NULL)
/* code to set pointers at the node to be */
/* deleted and its previous node */
   {
      if (t->n==num)
         break;
      prev = t;
      t = t-> next;
   }
   if (t = = NULL)
```

```
/* node to be deleted was not found in */
/* the list */
   printf ( "Number not found to be deleted" );
   prev->next = t->next;
/* code to reset the pointers */
   free(t);
/* delete the node permanently */
}
```

Searching in a linked list

This is one of the most commonly used functions in a linked list. This function is implemented by traversing from the beginning of the list to the end to search for a node with a given number. If the number is found, the pointer to that node is returned else NULL is returned.

Searching in a linked list

```
node* search(int num)
{
   node* t
   t = top;
while (t != NULL)
/* loop to search for a given number in the */
/* linked list */
{
   if (t->n == num)
   return t;
   t = t->next;
}
return NULL;
```

9 File Processing and Pre Processor Directives

> Since most of the times you would be working on the data from the files on the system, it is important to read this chapter.

File Handling

By now, reading from the standard input and writing to the standard output would be a very common task. Now, let's take a look at a totally different area, accessing files from programs. Files are nothing but just stream of bytes. There are two types of files. They are text files and binary files. Often, situations would arise when it will be necessary to read and write into files rather than standard input/ output. To give a few examples, the programs like copying one file to another, renaming a file, etc., perform a lot of file handling operations.

To start off, here are the basic steps to follow, to handle files in your program:

1. Declare a file pointer.
2. Open the file through your program and assign the file pointer to it.
3. Manipulate the contents of the file, through the file pointer.
4. It is possible to read and write into the file.
5. After all the work is done, close the file through your program.

The following sections will give you the syntax and define the way the above- mentioned steps have to be done.

The FILE Pointer

Before you open a file, you have to declare a file pointer. This will point to the structure containing the details of the file that you open. The declaration of the file pointer is done in the following way:

```
FILE *fp;
```

Here, fp is declared as a pointer to the type FILE. The file pointer need not necessarily point to the beginning of the file. It is possible to position the file pointer to user-defined positions using inbuilt functions provided by C.

File Accessing Functions

C provides inbuilt functions to access files in the standard library header file <stdio .h> . Discussing all, is not required for the beginner's level. So, let us analyze the very important and commonly used functions.

fopen ( ) function

To open a file through your program, fopen function can be used. The syntax is:

```
FILE* fopen(char *name, char* mode);
```

The first argument to this function is the name of the file that has to be opened. If the file is in the same directory as your program, it is enough to give the filename alone ("first.c") else it is required to give the full path along with the file name ("c \ \ first \ \ first.c "). Note, when you are providing just one back slash, the next character along with the back slash is taken as an escape sequence character. So, to avoid such interpretation, a back slash is to be proceeded with another back slash. The second argument is the mode in which the file is to be opened, i.e., whether you want to perform just read operation, just write operation or both. The following table gives the modes available and its purpose.

Modes and the operations allowed in fopen ( )

Modes	*Operations Possible*
"r"	open text file for reading
"w"	open text file for writing, previous contents discarded, if any
"a"	append; open or create file for writing at the end of the file
"r"	Open text file for update i.e., reading and writing
"w+"	create or open text file for update; discard previous contents, if any
"a+"	append; open or create text file for update, writing at the end.

This fopen function returns the pointer to the file structure. So, the file pointer declared must be assigned to it.

For example,

```
fp = fopen("first.c","r");
```

```
/* fp is pointing to file that is opened in read
            mode */
```

feof ( ) function

While manipulating a file, it is often required to know when we have reached the end of the file. This function returns non-zero integer when the end of the file is reached. The syntax of this function is:

```
int feof(FILE* fp);
```

The following loop gives the way the file can be manipulated until end of file is reached.

```
while (! feof(fp)
{
/*....*/
}
```

C also provides a macro EOF, which recognizes the end of a file. EOF is a #defined macro in < stdio.h> , commonly defined as -1.

fclose ( ) function

After, all the work has been done on the file, we have to disengage it from our program. In simple words, the file needs to be closed. fclose function does this operation. This function frees the file pointer and empties the buffer used. For every file open operation, this function is called automatically when a program terminates normally. But it is recommended that this function is called explicitly. The prototype for this function is:

```
int fclose(FILE *filepointer);
```

For example,

```
fclose(fp) ; /*fp declared as file pointer */
```

Other File Manipulation Functions

To access the contents of the file, there are a set of functions used for various purposes The following sub-sections describe these functions in detail.

getc / fgetc function:

This function is the simplest way to read from a file opened through the program. It needs a file pointer as argument to know which file to read from. It reads character by character. The syntax of this function is:

```
int getc(FILE *fp) ;
```

This function returns the next character from the file pointed by fp and when the character is read, fp points to the next character of the file. To read all the contents of the file, this function can be used until we encounter an EOF. We also have a function fgetc, which is similar to this function. There are internal details that make these functions differ. Knowing these details is as of now out of scope.

putc/fputc function

This function is the simplest way to write into a file opened through the program. The file pointer specifies the file in which the character has to be written. It writes character by character. The prototype of this function is:

```
int putc(int c, FILE *fp);
```

This function returns the character c written into the file pointed by fp and an EOF in case of an error occurred while writing: fputc, is also similar toputc ( ) except for some internal details.

fgets and fputs functions

fgets has the following prototype:

```
char* fgets(char *s, int n, FILE *fp);
```

This function reads at most n -1 characters into the strings from the file pointed by fp. If a newline '\n ' is encountered before n -1 characters, reading is stopped at that point. The array s is terminated with a NUL character ('\0') automatically. This function is basically used to read line by line from a file.

fputs has the following prototype:

```
int fputs(const char *s, FILE *fp) ;
```

This function writes the string s into the file pointed by fp. It returns non-negative integer when the process is completed successfully else it returns EOF.

fscanf ( ) and fprintf ( ) functions

fscanf has the following format:

```
int fscanf(FILE *fp, const char* format, ...);
```

This function is similar to scanf except for that the operation is done on a file. That is, fscanf reads from the file pointed by fp under the control of the format string. fscanf returns the number of input items read. The function returns EOF in case of any errors.

fprintf has the following format:

```
int fprintf (FILE *fp, const char *format, ...);
```

This function is similar to printf except for that the operation is done on a file. That is, fprintf writes into the file pointed by fp under the control of the format string. It returns the number of characters written. The function returns a negative value in the case of any errors.

Program based on file handling

```
/***************************************************/
/* Program to read and write into files */
/***************************************************/
# include<stdio.h>
int main(void)
{
  FILE *fp_r, *fp_w;
  char c;
  char *str = "Hello world"
  int i = 0;

  fp_r = fopen("first.c","r");
/* opening a file in the reading mode */

c = getc(fp_r);
/* read a character from the file */

while(c!=EOF)
/* processing the loop till the end of file is */
/* reached. */
{
  printf("%c",c)
  c = getc(fp_r)
}

fclose(fp_r);
/* closing the file that has been opened */

fp_w = fopen("first.c","w");
/* opening a file in the writing mode */
c=putc(str[i], fp_w);
```

```
/* write a character to the file */
  i++;
  while(str[i] !='\0' )
/* processing till the end of the string to be */
/* written to the file is reached */
{
  c = putc(str[I], fp_w);
  i++;
  }
  fclose(fp_w)  ;
}
```

Direct input and output functions

C provides functions for direct input and output operations which are capable of reading input from a file and writing a stream of bytes into a file. Functions which perform these operations are:

1. fread ()
2. fwrite ( )

The prototype for fread function is:

```
size_t fread(void *ptr, size_t size_obj, size_t
           nobj, FILE* fp) ;
```

size_t is typedefed to unsigned int in <stddef.h>.

fread reads from fp into the array ptr at most nobj objects of size size_obj . It returns the number of objects successfully read. This number can also be less than the number of objects instructed to be read. feof and ferror can be used to find if the operation had failed. The syntax for the fwrite function is:

```
size_t fwrite(void *ptr, size_t size_obj, size_t
           nobj, FILE* fp) ;
```

fwrite writes from the array ptr , nobj number of objects of size size_obj to the file pointed by the fp. It returns the number of objects that have been written successfully. If the return value is less than nobj. then it indicates an error.

File Positioning Pointers

C provides the programmer with inbuilt functions that can be used to position the tile pointer to a desired position in the file. The file pointer position can also be retrieved by these functions.

ftell ( ) function

The prototype forftell is given below:

```
long ftell(FILE*fp)
```

This function returns the current file pointer's position in the file pointed by fp. It returns - 1L on error.

fgetpos ( ) function

The prototype for fgetpos is:

```
int fgetpos(FILE *fp, fops_t *ptr)
```

The type fops_t is a data type suitable for storing such values.

This function records the position of the file pointer pointed by fp in ptr .This can be used later to set back the pointer to the same place using fsetpos .On an error, a non-zero number is returned.

fseek ( ) function

The syntax of this function is:

```
int fseek(FILE *fp, long offset, int origin)
```

This function sets the file pointer fp to a position in the file. Any subsequent read or write operation will start from this position.

For a binary file, the position of the pointer is set offset characters from the origin. The origin can be either SEEK_SET (beginning of the file), SEEK_CUR (current position of the file pointer) or SEEK_END (end of the file).

For a text stream, offset must be zero or a value returned from ftell. fseek returns non-zero number on an error.

rewind ( ) function

The syntax of this function is:

```
void rewind(FILE *fp)
```

This function places the function pointer of a file to the beginning of the file. This is similar to the function performed by the following statements:

```
fseek(fp,0L,SEEK_SET);
```

fsetpos ( ) function

The syntax of this function is:

```
int fsetpos(FILE *fp, const fpost_t *ptr)
```

This function is used to set the position of the file pointer in a file. This is different from f seek as it does not provide any options but can only position the pointer to the position recorded by the fgetpos in *ptr. This function returns a non-zero on error.

C Preprocessor

Every program before compilation goes through a set of steps in the preprocessing state. Preprocessing takes place in several logical steps. In this stage, few sections of source files can be skipped, other source files can be included and macros can be substituted. These capabilities are called preprocessing, because they occur before compilation of the program. But, every C compiler does not necessarily follow these steps. (One of the major functions of a C preprocessor is Tokenizing (The program is split into tokens). The final step of the preprocessor is to link the resulting program with necessary programs and library.

Apart from these steps, the C preprocessor gives the user the flexibility to perform some tasks before compilation. Preprocessing directives are provided for this purpose. There are several preprocessing directives that the programmer can use. The preprocessing directives and their semantics are discussed in hte following sections.

#define directive

This directive has the following syntax:

```
define identifier substitution_token
```

This directive is used for mere text substitution. This substitution is otherwise known as call by name. Every occurrence of the identifier is substituted by the substitution_token. The primary advantage is that it increases the readability of the program.

For example,

```
# define TRUE 1
# define FALSE 0
```

Using TRUE and FALSE in the program would be more readable than using 1 and 0 in many places.

This directive can also be used as function-like directive. It can take arguments and perform some operation on it. The only difference between functions and this directive will be that there will not be any control transfer as in functions but only text substitution. For example,

```
# define INC (a) a+1
```

For every occurrence of INC (variable) , it will be substituted as:

```
variable + 1
```

include directive

This directive searches for a header or source file, which can be processed by the implementation, to be included in the program. The syntax for this directive is either:

```
# include <filename>
```

or:

```
# include <filename>
```

In both these cases, the statements are replaced by the contents of the file named filename. The difference of using " " or <> I lies in the place where the filename is searched for. If " " is used, then the file is searched in the place of the source file else the file is searched in the general directory where the header files and library files are generally stored. This path is decided by the implementation. # include can be nested.

#undef directive

An identifier that has been #defined can be undefined using the following control line

```
# undef identifier
```

This statement causes the identifier's definition to be forgotten. If a undefined macro name is #undefed, the directive is ignored.

Conditional compilation

C Preprocessor also equips the programmer with the facility to conditionally include sections of code in a program during compile-time.

#if, #elif, #else and endif

A prototype of the directive is given below:

```
#if condition
text
#elif condition (optional)
text
#else condition(optional)
text
#endif line
```

These directives are similar to if – else statement and serve the purpose of conditional inclusion of code sections.

The "if condition" is evaluated first. On returning a non-zero number, the immediately appearing text is processed else the "elif" or "else" part is included for compilation. The end of this conditional inclusion directive is indicated by the "#endif" line. The "#endif" directive identifies the end of the process of conditional inclusion. "#endif" is compulsory when "#if" is used.

For example,

```
#define MAX 40
#if MAX > 80
   #define MIN 80
#elif MAX < 0
   #define MIN 0
#else
   #define MIN 50
#endif
```

Here as MAX is 40, no conditions satisfy. It is not greater than 80 to enter the first block and it is not less than zero to enter into the "elif" block. finally, it reaches the "else" part and MIN is defined to 50.

#ifdef and #ifndef

The #ifdef and #ifndef allows the programmer to check if any macro has been defined previously or not. #ifdef checks if the given identifier is defined as macro. If it finds a macro definition the corresponding block is included for compilation, else the block is skipped #ifndef checks if a particular identifier is not defined as macro. If it is not defined then the corresponding block is included for compilation, else the block is skipped.

The following examples would help you know them better.

```
#define MAX 100
#ifdef MAX
   #define MIN 80
#endif
```

Since MAX is defined, MIN is defined to 80.

```
#define MAX 100
#ifndef MIN
   #define MIN 80
```

```
#endif
```

Since MIN is not defined, the block is not processed. Refer to the following example for a program using all the above given directives.

Preprocessing directives

```
/*************************************************/
/* Program to find greatest of two numbers using
        macros */
/*************************************************/
# include<stdio.h>
/* directive to include source or header files */
# define ARR_VAL 30
/* defining the value of MAX as 30 */
/* define BIG(a,b) (a > b ? a : b)
/* Macro with arguments to find the largest of 2
        numbers */
#finder VAL_A
#define VAL_A 100
# endif
/* Here first VAL_A is checked if it is not
        defined */
/* As it is not, it is defined to 100 */
# if def VAL_B
#define VAL_B 200
#endif
/* VAL_B is checked to be defined. As it is not,
        the */
/* else part is executed and VAL_B is defined to
        200 */
#undef VAL_C
/* Here VAL_C is not at all defined as per previous
        */
/* set of directives. so this statement is ignored
        by */
/* the preprocessor. */
int main (void)
{
int val = 0;
val = BIG(VAL_A, VAL_B);
```

```
/* First VAL_A is substituted as 100 and VAL_B as
          200 */
/* Next BIG is substituted as 100 > 200 ? 100 :
          200 */
/* This returns 200 which is assigned to val */
printf ( "%d", val);
/* Prints 200
}
```

10 TURBO C

> Turbo C is one of the popular compiler of C though there are others too in the market.

Introduction

Turbo C is one compiler of C. It is helps you in compiling your C program in the following ways.

1. It is a tradional C command line system in which the functionf of editing, compiling, linking, and executing a program are invoked from the operating system as separate programs. This system is relatively inefficient. Though, it must be used in certain complex situations, such as linking you C code with a code written in assembly language.

2. The second method for creating programs in Turbo C's Integrated Development Environment (IDE). Users of Turbo Pascal and Turbo Basic must be familiar with major features of the IDE. In this environment, all the necessary operations for program development are available in a unified screen display with menus and windows. The IDE provides an ideal environment for learning C.

Working with Turbo C

To start IDE, enter TC at the DOS prompt and you will see the figure shown on the next page.

Various menus on this screen are explained below.

File Menu

The following commands are listed under this.

Load	It prompts you for a file name and then loads that file into the editor.
Pick	It displays a menu that contains a list of the files (maximum of 9) that you load into the environment. You can use up or down arrow key to select a file to load and press Enter key.

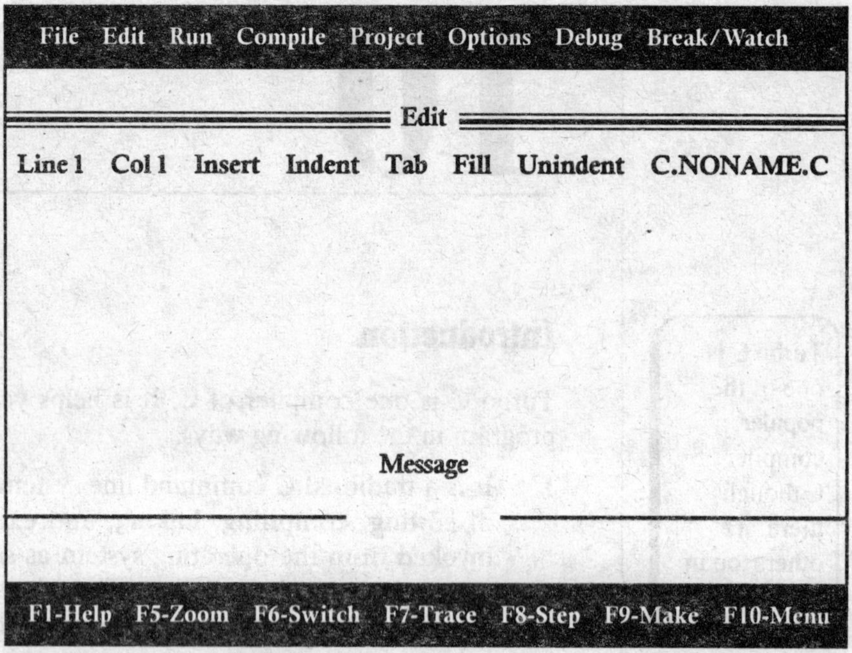

New	It erases the current contents of the editor and lets you edit a new file. If the previous file has been changed but not saved to disk, it will prompt you to first save the file before erasing it. The new file is named NONAME.C by default.
Save	It saves the current file in he ditor to disk. If you have edited a new file called NONAME.C it will prompt you to change its name if you desire.
Write to	It lets you save entire file or select portion of the current file in the editor to a different file name.
Directory	It displays the contents of the current working directory. You can specify the mask or use default *.* mask.
Change dir	It displays the path name of the current working directory and allows you to chnage to another if you desire.
OS Shell	It loads the DOS command processor and lets you execute DOS commands. After executing the DOS command(s), type EXIT to return to the Turbo C's IDE.
Quit	It quits Turbo C's IDE.

Run Menu

Run	It executes the current program. If the program has not been yet compiled, the program will be compiled first.
Program reset	It terminates a program being run in a debug mode and allows you to re-run your program from the beginning.
Go to cursor	It executes your program until it reaches the line of code where the cursor is positioned.
Trace into	It executes the next statement. If that statement includes a function call, the function will be traced into.
Step over	It executes the next line of code, but does not trace into any function that is called.
User screen	It lets you view the output produced by your program.

Compile Menu

Compile to OBJ	It allows you to compile the current file in the editor to an .OBJ file, which is a relocatable object file that is ready to be linked into an .EXE file that can be executed.
Make EXE file	It compiles your program and then links it to create an executable file.
Link EXE file	It links the current .OBJ and library files.
Build all	It recompiles and links all files in a project whether they are modified or not.
Primary C file	It lets you specify a primary file to be compiled instead of the one that is currently loaded into the editor.
Get info	It displays information about the current session.

Project Menu

Project Name	It lets you specify the name of a project file that contains the names of the files that make up the project. These files are then compiled,

	if necessary, and linked together to form the final executable program. For example, if the project file contains the file names file1.c, file2.c, and file3.c, all three files will be compiled and linked to form the executable code named file1.exe. All project files must have the extension .RJ.
Break make on	It lets you specify what type of conditions cause a make to stop. Ypou can specify to stop the make on warning, errors, fatal erros, on before linking.
Auto dependencies	It causes Turbo C to automatically re-create files that depend on other files that have changed.
Clear project	It removes the project file name from the system and resets the message window.
Remove messages	It clears the message window.

Options Menu

This is further divided into 7 sub menus.

- Compiler
- Linker
- Environment
- Directories
- Arguments
- Save options
- Retrieve options

Let us see what each one of them contains.

Compiler Submenu

Model	It allows you to select which memory model is to be used to compile your programs. The deault is small, which is adequate for most applications.
Defines	It allows you to define temporary pre-processor symbols to be used automatically by your

program. You can define one or more macros by separating them with semicolons. This feautre is useful during development and debugging.

Code generation Selecting Code generation presents you with a large number of switches that you can set. These switches are:

Calling conventions You can choose between the C calling conventions and the Pascal calling conventions. a calling convention is simply the method by which functions are called and arguments are passed. Generally, you should use the C calling convention.

Instruction set By default, Turbo C compiler used 8086/8088 instruction set. However, you can change the processor.

Floating point It allows you to control the way Turbo C implements floating point operations. The default and most common method is to use 8087/80287 emulation routines. The 8087 chip is the math coprocessor for 8088 family of CPU's, while 80287 is the mathc coprocessor for 80286 CPU. When these coprocesors are int he system, they allow very rapid floating point operations. However, if you don't have a math coprocessor or if your program will be used on variety of computers, the 8087's operation must be emulated in software, which is much slower. The emulation mode uses the math coprocessor by default if one is in the system, or calls the emulation routines if no math coprocessor is installed. If you don't know that math coprocessor is present in every system on which the program will run, you can select 8087/ 80287 option, which generate in-line 8087/80287 code. this is the fastest way to implement floating-point operations. Finally, you can deselct floating-point altogether when your program does not use it, thereby allowing the object code to be much smaller.

Default char type	It determines whether the type char is signed or unsigned. By default, char is signed in Turbo C.
Alignment	It determines whether data is aligned on byte or word boundaries. On the 8086 and 80286 processors, memory accesses are quicker if data is word aligned. However, there is no difference on the 8088. The default is byte-alignment.
Generate underbars	On the default, determine whether an underscore is added to the start of each identifier in the link file. You should not turn this off unless you are an experienced programmer and understand the inner working of Turbo C.
Merge duplicate strings	Off by default. By setting it on, the Turbo C compiler can be instructed to merge identical strings into one string, the result being smaller programs.
Standard stack frame	On by default, it is used to force Turbo C compiler to generate standard calling and returning code for each function call to help in debugging.
Test stack overflow	By setting it on, forces Turbo C compiler to check for stack overflow. This makes the program to run slower, but it may be necessary in order to find certain bugs. If your program crashes inexplicably from time to time, you might want to compile it with this test turned on to see if stack overflows are the problem.
Line number	On by default, with this you can force

Turbo C compiler to enter the number of each line of the source into the object file. This is useful when using a debugger.

OBJ debug information — It controls whether debugging information is compiled into your file. This information is necessary when you are using a debugger.

Optimization — This option has four switches.

Optimize for — Turbo C compiler is very efficient, but for some reasons, the optimations that makes the object code smaller also makes it slower. Other optimizations make the object code faster but larger. Turbo C compiler lets you decide whether you want to optimize for speed or size by using this option. The default is size.

Use register ovariables — Turning it off, suppresses the use of register variables. Unless you are interfacing to non-Turbo C code, leave this option on.

Jump optimization — By setting on, you can make Turbo C compiler to rearrange the code within loops and switch statements. This can cause higher performance. However, if you are using a debugger on your object code, turn this off.

Source — The source option lets you set the number of significant characters in an identifier, determine whether comments can be nested, and force Turbo C to accept any the ANSI keywords. By default, Turbo C identifiers have 32 significant characters. However, you can set this number anywhere in the range 1 to 32. Turbo C supports the ANSI standard, but it has added various enhancements to the language to support the 8086 processor better. If you want to make sure that you are writing code that uses only the ANSI standard, toggle the option ANSI keywords only. Otherwise, leave it in its default(off) position. Nested comments - by setting this feature on, you can tell the Turbo C compiler to handle nested comments. By default nested comments are not permitted.

Errors

The error options lets you determine how errors are reported during the compilation process. There are 7 options in this menu. These are:

Errors:stop after — Let you specify after how many errors the compilation process must stop. The default is 25.

Warning:stop after — Lets you specify after how many warnings the compilation process must stop. The default is 100.

Display warnings — Turbo C is very forgiving and tries to make sense out of your source code no matter how unusual it may seem. However, if Turbo C has a suspicion that wheat you have written is incorect, it displays a warning message. A warning error does not stop compilation; it simply inform you of Turbo C's concerns over a certain construct. It is for you to decide whether Turbo C is correct in its concern.

Portability errors — Several types of errors can be generated. The first are portability errors, which reflect coding methods that would render the program non-portable to another type of processor.

ANSI violations — These types of warnings are generated because of non ANSI code practices.

Common errors — This category consists of common programming errors.

Less common errors — This category consists of less common programming errors.

Names

The names option lets you change the names Turbo C compiler uses for the various memory segments used by your program. You will need to change these only in unusual situations. Don't change the names unless you are an experienced assembly language programmer and know what you are doing.

Linker Submenu

The linker option has further 7 options.

Map file — By default, the Turbo C does not create a map file of your compiled program. a map file shows the relative positions of the variables and functions that make up your program and where they reside in memory. You may need to create a map file for debugging certain programs in complex situations. You can create a map file in 3 ways:

1. shows only segments,
2. shows global symbols, and
3. detailed map.

Initialize segments — By default off. By setting it on in highly special situations to force the linker to initialize the segments, but this is seldom necessary.

Default libraries — It applies only when you are linking modules compiled by other C compilers. By default this option is off. If you turn it on, the linker searches the libraries defined in the separately compiled modeules befoe searching Turbo C libraries.

Graphics library — By default on, and causes Turbo C compiler to search GRAPHICS.LIB library automatically when linking your program. This enables you to use Turbo C graphics functions. If you are not using graphic function, you can speed up the linking process, by setting it off.

Warn duplicate symbols — By defaulton, and causes the linker to warn you if you have defined duplicate global identifiers. But turning it off, you don't see this message and the linker chooses which one to use.

Stack warning

If you are using Turbo C to create routines to link with external assembly language routines, you might receive the link-time message No stack specified. You can eliminate this message by turning it off.

Case sensitive link

On by default because C is case-sensitive. However, if you are trying to link Turbo C modules with FORTRAN modules, for example, you may need to turn this option off.

Environment Options

Here you can change the way Turbo C's integrated environment works. This option has further eight options. These are:

Message tracking

By default, Turbo C displays the errors found in the current file loaded in the editor. However, you can tell it to track messages in all files related to a program or no to track errors at all by toggling it.

Keep messages

By default off, and error messages are cleared before each recompilation. By turning it on, older messages are retained and new one are added to the list.

Config auto save

When on, any changes made to the configuration file are automatically saved each time you run a program, use OS shell command or exit Turbo C. If it off, the configuration is saved only on your command. This option is off by default.

Edit auto save

When on, the editor automatically saves the current file to disk each time you run the program, use the OS shell command. If it is off, the file is saved when you specify ask. It is off by default.

Backup files

On by default, and when you save a file. Turbo C automatically renames the previous version of that file from a .C extension to a .BAK extension. In this way, you always have the previous version as a backup.

Tab size

Default tab size is 8, you can change here.

Zoomed windows	If on, the active window occupies the entire screen. By default this option is off.
Screen size	If you have EGA or VGA video adapter, you can tell Turbo C compiler to use a 43-line display. If you have VGA, you can use 50-line display. These settings are specified using this option. A 25-line display is used by default.

Directories Submenu

This option has 5 entries.

Include directories	You can specify a list of directories to be searched for you include files. The list can be up to 127 characters long, and the file names must be separated by semicolons.
Library directories	You can specify a list of directories to be searched for you library files. The list can also be up to 127 characters long, and the file names must be separated by semicolons.
Otuput directory	You can specify the directory used for output. The file and path name must not be longer than 63 characters.
Turbo C directory	You can specify here, where Turbo C looks for its help files and the TCCONFIG.TC file. The file and path name must not be longer than 63 characters.
Pick file name	You can specify here the path for pick files.

Arguments Submenu

As you know, when you run a program in the IDE, you do not type the program name as you do from the DOS prompt. Hence, it is not possible to specify the command line arguments directly when running a program in IDE.

By using this option, you can enter command-line arguments required by your program. Then, each time you run the program, the command-line arguments you specify will be used.

Saving and Retrieve Submenu

Once you have customized Turbo C by changing various options, you have two choices. You can use your chosen options during your current session only, or you can save them. The two entries save options and retrieve options allow you to save and load the options.

Debug Menu

The debug option lets you perform various debugging operations and set various debugging options. The Debug option has furhter 6 sub options. These are:

Evaluate	It allows you to view or alter the value of any variable or expression in your program. However, the expression cannot include funcation calls or macros.
Call stack	It displays the functions that have been called, but not yet returned, in stack-wise order. In other words, it displays the call stack, meaning that the most recently called function is on top of the stack and the least recently called function is on the bottom.
Find function	It displays the source code of the function that you specify. The function source code must be available to Turbo C.
Refresh display	It redisplays the Turbo C IDE screen. This option is useful if an application program overwrites the IDE screen.
Display swapping	It lets you determine how the screen switches between the IDE screen and the user screen.
Source debugging	It lets you include debugging information in the executable form of your program. You need to include debugging information in your program if you want to use Turbo C's debugger.

Breake and Watch Menu

This option is a part of Turbo C debugger. It lets you specify various expressions to watch while your program is executing. It also lets you manage breakpoints. A breakpoint is a location you define in your program at which execution stops.

The Break/watch option has further 7 sub options. They are:

Add watch	It allows you to add a variable or expression to

	the watch whose value is to be displayed during execution of the program. There are two restrictions to watched expressions; they cannot include function calls or macro names.
Delete watch	It allows you to remove current watched expressions.
Edit watch	It lets you modify the highlighted watched expressions.
Remove all watches	It removes all watched expressions.
Toggle breakpoint	It lets you alternatively set or clear a breakpoint.
Clear all breakpoints	It clears all breakpoints set previously in your program.
View next breakpoint	It positions the cursor voer the location of the next breakpoint in your program.

Keyboard Shorcuts

Activate Edit option to get the Turbo C's built-in editor.

Commands for Moving Around Your File

Key combination	*Description*
Ctrl + E or ↑	Moves the cursor one line up.
Ctrl + X or ↓	Moves the cursor one line down.
Ctrl + S or ←	Moves the cursor one character to the left.
Ctrl + D or →	Moves the cursor one character to the right.
Ctrl + A or Ctrl + ←	Moves the cursor to the beginning of the current or preceding word.
Ctrl + F or Ctrl + →	Moves the cursor to the beginning of the next word.
Ctrl + Q + S or Home	Moves the curosr to the beginning of the file.
Ctrl + Q + D or End	Moves the cursor to the end of the file.
Ctrl + R or PgUp	Moves the cursor to the top of the screen.
Ctrl + C or PgDn	Moves the cursor to the bottom of the screen.

Ctrl + PgUp	Moves the cursor to the beginning of the file.
Ctrl + PgDn	Moves the cursor to the end of the file.
Ctrl + Home	Moves the cursor to the top line of the screen, remaining in the current column.
Ctrl + End	Moves the cursor to the bottom line of the screen remaining in the current column.

Commands for Inserting and Deleting Text

Key combination	*Description*
Ctrl + V	Toggles between insert and overwrite mode.
Ctrl + N	Inserts a blank line at the current cursor position, pushing lines downward in the file.
Ctrl + G or Del	Delets the character at the current cursor position. Characters to the right of the deleted character move leftword to fill in the vacant spot.
Ctrl + H or Backspace	Deletes the character preceding the one at the current cursor position. Characters to the right of the deleted character move leftword to fill in the vacant spot.
Ctrl + Y	Deletes the current line.
Ctrl + Q + Y	deletes from the current cursor position to the end of the current line.
Ctrl + T	Deletes from the current cursor position to the ed of the current word.
Ctrl + E or Alt + Backspace	Undo the last movement of deletion action.

Commands for Manipulating Blocks of Text

Key combination	*Description*
Ctrl + K + B	Marks the beginning of a block of text.
Ctrl + K + K	Marks the end of a block of text.
Ctrl + K + C	Copies the marked block of text at current cursor position.
Ctrl + K + V	Moves the marked block from its position to the current cursor position.

Ctrl + K + Y	Deletes the marked block of text.
Ctrl + K + W	Write the marked block of text to a new file whose name you have to specify. The IDE assumes that this file has a .C extension unless you specify.
Ctrl + K + R	Reads the contents of a file and inserts at the current cursor position. You have to specify the file whose contents you want to copy.
Ctrl + K + P	Prints the marked block of text.
Ctrl + K + H	To hide/deactivate the marked block of text. The block can again be activated by repeating the key combination.

Commands for Finding and Replacing Text

Key combination	*Description*
Ctrl + Q + F or Alt + S + F	Searches a specified string.
Ctrl + Q + A or Alt + S + R	Searches a specified string and replaces it with a second string also be specified.
Ctrl + L	Repeat the last Find or Find and Replace command.

Hot keys

The Tubro C IDE contains several hot keys, which are shorhand for menu selections. Several hot keys are shown as reference line at the bottom of the screen, these are default. The complete list is given below.

Hot Keys

Key combination	*Description*
F1	Activate the on-line help system.
F2	Save the file currently being edited.
F3	Loads a file.
F4	Execute program until cursor is reached.
F5	Zoom the window.
F6	Switch between windows.

F7	Trace into function calls.
F8	Trace, but skip function calls.
F9	Compile and link a program.
F10	Toggle between the main menu and the editor.
Alt + F1	Last help screen.
Alt + F3	Pick a file to load.
Alt + F5	Switch between user screen and IDE.
Alt + F6	Switch between watch and message window.
Alt + F7	Previous error.
Alt + F8	Next error.
Alt + F9	Compile file to .OBJ.
Alt + C	Activate the compile menu.
Alt + D	Activate the debug menu.
Alt + E	Activate the editor.
Alt + F	Activate the file menu.
Alt + O	Activate the options menu.
Alt + P	Activate the project menu.
Alt + R	Activate the run menu.
Alt + X	Quit Turbo C IDE.
Ctrl + F1	Request help about the item that contains the cursor.
Ctrl + F2	Reset program.
Ctrl + F3	Show function call stack.
Ctrl + F4	Evaluate an expression.
Ctrl + F7	set a watch expression (debugging).
Ctrl + F8	Set or clear a breakpoint.
Ctrl + F9	Execute the current program.

Quitting Turbo C IDE

You can quit from Turbo C compiler at any time by first selecting File menu and the Quit from File submenu or by pressing Alt+X at any time. If the current file is not saved, then it will prompt you to save it and then exists.

11 Projects in C

Calendar

This is a calendar program which displays the calendar of month wise and you can find any calendar date as after typing the month and year.

This program manage two types of calendar options as :

1. To see calendar of particular month
2. Get day of date

If you will choose the menu option 1 then, you will see the a screen will appear for inputting the day, month and year prompt for displaying the calendar. Also, with this option it validates the date, which you entered. Finally you will see the calendar in a tabular form, which you want.

If you will choose the menu option 2 then, you will see the a screen will appear for inputting the day, month and year prompt for displaying the character day of inputted date.

The menu program (Menu.C).

```
int menu(void)
{
   int z;
   int option;
   clrscr();
   window(1,1,80,25);
   textbackground(WHITE);
   clrscr();
   window(61,7,62,21);
   textbackground(0);
   clrscr();
   window(7,20,62,21);
```

```
textbackground(0);
clrscr();
window(5,5,60,20);
textbackground(4);
textcolor(10);
clrscr();

gotoxy(1,1);   //196
printf
("ÚÄÄÄÄÄÄÄÄÄÄÄÄÄÄÄÄÄÄÄÄÄÄÄÄÄÄÄÄÄÄÄÄÄÄÄÄ
        ÄÄÄÄÄÄÄÄÄÄÄÄÄÄÄÄÄÄxÄÄ¿");
gotoxy(1,16);
printf
("ÀÄÄÄÄÄÄÄÄÄÄÄÄÄÄÄÄÄÄÄÄÄÄÄÄÄÄÄÄÄÄÄÄÄÄÄÄÄ
        ÄÄÄÄÄÄÄÄÄÄÄÄÄÄÄÄÄÄÄÄÄÄÄÄÄ¾");

for(  z=2;z<16;z++)
{
   gotoxy(1,z);
   printf  ("³");
   gotoxy(56,z);
   printf  ("³");
}
gotoxy(14,4);
printf ("M A I N   M E N U");
gotoxy(12,5);
printf  ("=====================");
gotoxy(10,7);
printf  (" 1  :: To see calendar of particular
        month ");
gotoxy(10,9);
printf (" 2 :: Get day of date");
gotoxy(10,11);
gotoxy(10,13);
printf (" 3 :: Exit");
gotoxy(20,15);
```

```
   printf (" Your option    ");
   option = getch ()-48; // sub to ascii
   printf ("%d",option);
   return (option);
}
```

The source program for getting day of any date from 1 AD onwards. (Day.C)

```
/* Do not compile this file */

//  Program only gives the day of any date from 1
          A.D. to __

#include<stdlib.h>

int flag_leap;
int flag_day;
int option;

int firstday;
int loop_size;
int call_day;
date(void)      ///consturtor
{
   flag_leap=0;flag_day=30;call_day=0;clrscr();
}
//————————————
int user_date, user_mth, user_year;
int call_day;
int input_data(int option);
int check_date();
int day(void);
//——————————
void screen(void)
{
   clrscr();
```

```
    window(4,4,60,10);
    textbackground(2);
    textcolor(4);
    clrscr();
}
//_______________
/* This function is used to the date, month and
            year to find the calender and return
            month to the main program */
int   input_data(int option)
{

    //clrscr();///in case color remove this line
    screen();

    if  (option==2)
    {
       printf ("\n\tEnter Date    :: ");
       scanf  ("%d",&user_date);
    }
    else
    {
       user_date=1;
    }
    printf ("\n\tEnter Month    ::  ");
    scanf  ("%d",&user_mth);
    monthnum=user_mth-1;
    printf ("\n\tEnter Year  ::  ");
    scanf ("%d",&user_year);
    return  (monthnum);
}  //  date::input_data

/* This function is used to check the date validity,
            which you entered through the input_data
            function. */
```

```
int check_date(void)
{
   ///for leap year
   int cent;//century year
   int ch;
   if (user_date<1 || user_date>31||user_mth<1
         ||user_mth >12 ||user_year<=0)  //if
         date 0 or any -ive
   {
      screen();
      printf (" **** ERROR  \n\tInvalid date ");
      if (user_date<1)
         printf ("\n\tDate less than 1");
      if (user_date>31)
         printf ("\n\tDate greater than 31");
      if (user_mth<1)
         printf ("\n\tMonth less than 1");
      if (user_mth>12)
         printf ("\n\tMonth greater than 12");
      if (user_year<=0)
         printf ("\n\tNOT VAILD FOR B.C. dates!!");
      printf ("\n\n\tWana try again \n\t\tPress 1
            else any key");

      ch=getch();
      if (ch==49)  //ascii 1
      {
         monthnum = input_data( option);//want to
            enter again so call input function
         check_date();// clrscr();
      }
      else
         exit(0);
   }
   if (user_year%4==0)  //leap year
   {  ///  if(user_year%4==0)
```

```
if  (user_year%100==0)        ///century  leap
        year
{
    cent= user_year/100;
    if  (cent%4==0)
        flag_leap=1;
    else
        flag_leap=0;
} //if century year
else                         //**non-century leap
        year
    flag_leap=1;
} //if leap year
if
(user_mth==1||user_mth==3||user_mth==5||user_mth==7|
        |user_mth==8||user_mth==10||user_mth==12)
        // month day 31's
    flag_day=31;
if  (user_mth==4||user_mth==6||user_mth==9|
        |user_mth==11)  // month day 31's
    flag_day=30;
if (user_mth==2 && flag_leap==1)       // month
        day 29's
    flag_day=29;
if (user_mth==2 && flag_leap==0)       // month
        day 28's
    flag_day=28;

switch (flag_day)
{  //switch
    case 28 :
    {
        if  (user_date>28)
            printf ("Invalid date!!");
        else
        {
            loop_size=28;
```

```
        call_day=1;
      } //else
      break;
    } //case 28
    case 29 :
    {
      if  (user_date>29)
        printf ("Invalid date!!");
      else
      {
        loop_size=29;
        call_day=1;
      } //else
      break;
    } //case 29
    case 30 :
    {
      if (user_date>30)
        printf ("Invalid date!!");
      else
      {
        loop_size=30;
        call_day=1;
      } //else
      break;
    } //case 30
    case 31 :
    {
      if (user_date>31)
        printf ("Invalid date!!");
      else
      {
        loop_size=31;
        call_day=1;
      } //else
```

```
        break;
      } //case 31
    }//switch
    return(loop_size);
}
//————————————————
int day(void)
{
    int odd_day=0;
    int yr_fst=0,yr_lst=0; //year_first, year_last
    int odd_day1=0;
    yr_fst=user_year/100; // quotient  no. of
           centuries
    yr_lst=user_year%100; // reminder

    odd_day= (yr_fst*100)+ (24 * yr_fst) + (yr_fst/
           4);
    //century +century contains 24 leap year +leap
           century year like 400,800..

    odd_day1= (yr_lst-1)+ ((yr_lst-1)/4);
    //total yr-1i.e for 1999 see 98 after century
           +leap years
    if(odd_day1>0)  //2000
       odd_day= odd_day+odd_day1;

    odd_day=odd_day+user_date;

    //last year   +   total leap year +    date
    switch (user_mth)
    { // switch
       case 1: odd_day+=0;break;
       case 2: odd_day+=3;break;
       case 3: odd_day+=3;break;
       case 4: odd_day+=6;break;
       case 5: odd_day+=8;break;
```

```
        case 6: odd_day+=11;break;
        case 7: odd_day+=13;break;
        case 8: odd_day+=16;break;
        case 9: odd_day=+19;break;
        case 10: odd_day+=21;break;
        case 11: odd_day+=24;break;
        case 12: odd_day+=26;break;
    } //switch
    ///leap yrs & non leap centuries yrs
    if (user_mth>2 && yr_lst!=0 && yr_lst%4==0)
        {odd_day++;}
    if (user_mth>2 && yr_lst==0 && yr_fst%4==0 )
        {odd_day—;}
    if (user_mth<3 && yr_lst==0 && yr_fst%4==0 )
        {odd_day=odd_day-2;}

    odd_day = odd_day%7;
    firstday=odd_day;
    return(odd_day);
} //date::day
```

The following is the source code of the main program.

```
// Shows calendar of month
#include <conio.h>
#include <stdio.h>
#include <stdlib.h>
# include <graphics.h>
int monthnum=0;
int firstday;// day num of first day of month
int loop_size;
int option ;//option from menu

#include "menu.c"
#include "day.c"

/* This function shows the calendar of the inputted
```

```
        date
*/
void show_calendar(void)
{
    char *month[12]={"JANUARY","FEBRUARY",
            "MARCH","APRIL","MAY","JUNE",
           "JULY","AUGUST","SEPTEMBER","OCTOBER",
            "NOVEMBER","DECEMBER"};
    //                 0   1     2     3    4
                5  6
    char *day[8]= {"Sun","Mon","Tues","Wed"
            ,"Thur","Fri","Sat"};
    int i=0;
    clrscr();
    printf                ("\n\n\n\t\t\t\t%s
            %d",month[monthnum],user_year,"\n\n\t");
    printf ("\n\n\n\t");
    // print days mon ......
    for( i=0;i<7;i++)
    {
        printf ("%s",day[i]);
        printf ("\t");
    }
    // for formatting \n\n
    printf ("\n\n\t");
    // printf blank space till start of day
    for(i=0;i<firstday;i++)
        printf ("\t");

    for( i=1;i<=loop_size;i++)
    {
        printf ("%d",i);
        printf ("\t");
        firstday++;
        if(firstday%7==0)
        {
```

```
            printf  ("\n\t");
            firstday=0;
          } //if ends

      } //for ends
   } //fun show_calendar ends

   // The function is used to display the main screen
              of the calendar program

   void m_screen(void)
   {
      clrscr();
      window(4,4,60,20);
      textbackground(1);
      textcolor(4);
      clrscr();
   }
   // The exit screen of the calender menu
   void screen_scroll(void)
   {
      int i,i1;
      clrscr();
      gotoxy(1,8);
      printf ("Have  A Nice Day " );//name++;
      for( i=0;i<10000;i++)
        for( i1=0;i1<10000;i1++);
   }
   // Main menu programming logic started
   void main(void)
   {
      char ch = 'y';
      while ((ch == 'y') || (ch == 'Y'))
      {
        clrscr();
        option = menu();//calmenu.cpp
```

```
m_screen();
switch (option)
{
   case 1 :
      {
         monthnum = input_data(option);
         loop_size = check_date();
         firstday = day();
         show_calendar();
         break;
      } //case1 show calendar
   case 2 :
      {
        monthnum = input_data(option);
        loop_size = check_date();
        firstday = day();
        printf ("\n\n\n\t\tRequired Data ");
        printf ("\n\n\t DAY       ::");
        switch (firstday)
        { //switch
           case 0 : printf (" SUNDAY");break;
           case 1 : printf (" MONDAY");break;
           case 2 : printf (" TUESDAY");break;
           case   3   :   printf   ("
      WEDNESDAY");break;
           case   4   :   printf   ("
      THURSDAY");break;
           case 5 : printf (" FRIDAY");break;
           case   6   :   printf   ("
      SATURDAY");break;
        } // inner switch over
        break;
      }
   case 3 :
      {
        screen_scroll();
```

```
            exit(0);
        }
    } // outer switch over
    getch();
  }
  getch();
}  // END of main
```

Bricks Game

Bricks is a computer game which is played by the single player at a time. In this game a four layer of bricks is there and you have to knock out the brick by the ball to get the point.For each knock you get 5 points. You have maximum of four balls and each time you lose the ball 10 marks are deducted from your score. You have to catch the ball on the paddle which is appearing on the bottom on the screen and if you will not able the catch the ball on the paddle you lose the ball. For moving the paddle use left and right arrow key.

As the ball and paddle are to be moved throughtout the game, we first store their images in the memory using malloc() function which is used to allocate the memory. After this, the image at new coordinates is set erasing the previous location. When the ball reaches to the boundary it will pushed inside. This program is made for the graphics mode so we have to intialize the the graphic mode using initgraph() function before playing this game.When you start the game screen() function is invoked first which display the instruction related to the game along with the two options play or exit. If you want to play select play option then it ask for the level of the player. There are three level slow,medium and fast according to which the speed of the ball is assigned.

So, you can select any level according to your choice and after that the bricks are displayed on the screen using bricks() function and whenever you hit the ball corresponding ball is deleted using delbrick() function. Whenever you hit more than one brick at a time the message "Good Shot" is displayed on the screen.And when only one ball get remain a warning "Last Ball...carefull" is diaplayed on the screen to aleret you. Your score is displayed on the left bottom of the screen and balls remaining is displayed on the right bottom of the screen. Differnt sounds are provided using the bell() function at various places.

```
#include <stdio.h>
#include <conio.h>
```

```
#include <ctype.h>
# include <process.h>
# include <dos.h>
# include <stdlib.h>
# include <graphics.h>
# include <stdio.h>

# define NULL 0
# define YES 1
# define NO 0
#define ESC   0x1b    /* Define the escape key
        */

int MaxX, MaxY, MidX, MidY ;
int bri[5][20]  ;

int     GraphDriver;  /* The Graphics device
          driver*/
int     GraphMode;    /* The Graphics mode value
        */
double AspectRatio;  /* Aspect ratio of a pixel
          on the screen*/
int     MaxXX, MaxYY; /* The maximum resolution
          of the screen */
int     MaxColors; /* The maximum # of colors
          available */
int     ErrorCode;    /* Reports any graphics
          errors */
struct palettetype palette;     /* Used to read
          palette info*/

// Initialize the graphics mode
void Initialize(void);

// Display the last screen of bricks
void SayGoodbye(void);

// Establish the main window for the demo
void MainWindow(char *header);
```

```
// Display the message Press any key to continue
        at last screen
void StatusLine(char *msg);

// Draws a boarder line at last screen
void DrawBorder(void);

// Changes the text style
void changetextstyle(int font, int direction, int
        charsize);

// Welcome screen of bricks game
mainscreen();

// Instruction messages of bricks game
screen();

// To display the bricks (in square box) and
        paddles in rectangle form and bulbs
        rounded form bricks();

// Delete a bricks when bulb hit it
delbrick(int,int);

// Echoes different musics
bell(int);

int graphmode = CGAHI, graphdriver = CGA, level;

main()
{ .
   union REGS ii, oo ;

   int BallX, BallY, Base1, Base2, dx = 1, dy = -
        1, OldX, OldY ;
   int totallayer[5] = { 10, 20, 30, 40, 50 }, max
        = 50, layer = 4 ;
   int i, flag = 0, speed = 25, score = 0, chance
        = 4, areareq ;

   char *m1, *m2 ;
```

```
/* Function to initialise the graphics mode */
initgraph ( &graphdriver, &graphmode,
        "d:\turboc3 " ) ;
mainscreen();
initgraph ( &graphdriver, &graphmode,
        "d:\turboc3 " ) ;
/* get the maximum value of x and y coordinates
        of the screen */
MaxX = getmaxx() ;
MaxY = getmaxy() ;
/* finding the center of the screen */
MidX = MaxX / 2 ;
MidY = MaxY / 2 ;

/* create opening  screen and accept the level
        of the  player's  */
level = screen() ;

/* assign the  speed to ball as per the level
        chosen */
switch ( level )
{
   case 'M' :
   case 'm' :
      speed = 15 ;
      break ;

   case 'F' :
   case 'f' :
      speed = 10 ;
}

/* draw the four layer of bricks, the paddle
        and the ball */
rectangle ( 0, 0, MaxX, MaxY - 12 ) ;
bricks() ;
rectangle ( MidX - 25, MaxY - 7 - 12, MidX + 25,
        MaxY - 12 ) ;
floodfill ( MidX, MaxY - 1 - 12, 12 ) ;
```

```
circle ( MidX, MaxY - 13 - 12, 12 ) ;
floodfill ( MidX, MaxY - 10 - 12, 12 ) ;

/* memory allocation for storing the image of
        the paddle */
areareq = imagesize ( MidX - 12, MaxY - 18,
        MidX + 12, MaxY - 8 ) ;
m1 =((char*) malloc ( areareq )) ;

/* memory allocation for storing the image of
        the ball */
areareq = imagesize ( MidX - 25, MaxY - 7, MidX
        + 25, MaxY - 1 ) ;
m2 =((char *) malloc ( areareq ) );

/* if unable to alloacte the memory  */
if ( m1 == NULL || m2 == NULL )
{
   puts ( "Not Enough memory!!" ) ;
   exit ( 1 ) ;
}

/* image of the paddle and the ball is stored
        into allocated memory */
getimage ( MidX - 12, MaxY - 7 - 12 - 12 + 1,
        MidX + 12, MaxY - 8 - 12, m1 ) ;
getimage ( MidX - 25, MaxY - 7 - 12, MidX + 25,
        MaxY - 1 - 12, m2 ) ;

/* store current position of the paddle and
        ball */
Base1 = MidX - 25 ;
Base2 = MaxY - 7 - 12 ;
BallX = MidX - 12 ;
BallY = MaxY - 7 - 12 + 1 - 12 ;

/* display balls remaining ( initially 3 ) */
gotoxy ( 45, 25 ) ;
printf( "Balls :"  );
for ( i = 0 ; i < 3 ; i++ )
```

```
    {
        circle ( 515 + i * 35, MaxY - 5, 12 ) ;
        floodfill ( 515 + i * 35, MaxY - 5, 12 ) ;
    }

    /* display starting score */
    gotoxy ( 1, 25 ) ;
    printf( "Score:   ");
    gotoxy(16,25);
    printf("%d",score);

    /* select font and alignment for displaying
         text */
    settextjustify ( CENTER_TEXT, CENTER_TEXT ) ;
    changetextstyle ( GOTHIC_FONT, HORIZ_DIR, 4 )
         ;

    while ( 1 )
    {
        flag = 0 ;

        /* saving current x and y coordinates of the
             ball */
        OldX = BallX ;
        OldY = BallY ;

        /* update ballx and bally to move the ball
             in correct direction */
        BallX = BallX + dx ;
        BallY = BallY + dy ;

        /* according to the position of ball the
             layer of bricks is determined */
        if ( BallY > 40 )
        {
            max = 50 ;
            layer = 4 ;
        }
        else
        {
```

```
if ( BallY > 30 )
{
   max = 40 ;
   layer = 3 ;
}
else
{
   if ( BallY > 20 )
   {
      max = 30 ;
      layer = 2 ;
   }
   else
   {
      if ( BallY > 10 )
      {
         max = 20 ;
         layer = 1 ;
      }
      else
      {
         max = 10 ;
         layer = 0 ;
      }
   }
}
}

/* if the ball hits the right boundary, move
     it to the left */
if ( BallX > ( MaxX - 24 - 1 ) )
{
   bell ( 5 ) ;
   BallX = MaxX - 24 - 1 ;
   dx = -dx ;
}

/* if the ball hits the left boundary, move
     it to the right */
```

```
if ( BallX < 1 )
{
   bell ( 5 ) ;
   BallX = 1 ;
   dx = -dx ;
}

/* if the ball hits the top boundary, move
     it down */
if ( BallY < 1 )
{
   bell (  5 ) ;
   BallY = 1 ;
   dy = -dy ;
}

/* if the ball is in the area of the bricks
     */
if ( BallY < max )
{
   /* if there is no brick  at the top of the
     ball */
   if ( bri[layer][ ( BallX + 10 ) / 32 ] ==
     1 )
   {
      /*  if the ball touches a brick */
      for ( i = 1 ; i <= 6 ; i++ )
      {
         /* check whether there is a brick to
      the right of the ball */
         if ( bri[layer][ ( BallX + i + 10 )
      / 32 ] == 0 )
         {
            /* if there is a brick */
            BallX = BallX + i ;
            flag = 1 ;
            break ;
         }

         /* check whether there is a brick to
```

```
the left of the ball */
  if ( bri[layer][ ( BallX - i + 10 )
/ 32 ] == 0 )
  {
    BallX = BallX - i ;
    flag = 1 ;
    break ;
  }
}

/* if the ball does not touch a brick
at the top, left or right */
if ( !flag )
{
  /* check if the ball has moved above
the current layer */
  if ( BallY < totallayer[layer - 1] )
  {
    /* if so, change current layer
appropriately */
    layer-- ;
    max = totallayer[layer] ;
  }

  /* restore the image of the ball at
the old coordinates */
  putimage ( OldX, OldY, m1, OR_PUT )
;

  /* erase the image at the old
coordinates */
  putimage ( OldX, OldY, m1, XOR_PUT )
;

  /* place the image of the ball at
the new coordinates */
  putimage ( BallX, BallY, m1, XOR_PUT
) ;

  /* delay for fewseconds*/
  delay ( speed ) ;
```

```
        /* carry on moving the ball */
        continue ;
    }
}

/* when ball touch the brick control comes
   to this point */
bell ( 5 ) ; /* play music */

/* erase the touched brick  */
delbrick ( ( BallX + 10 ) / 32, layer ) ;

/* if the brick hit is on the extreme
   right */
if ( ( BallX + 10 ) / 32 == 19 )
    line ( MaxX, 0, MaxX, 50 ) ;  /* redraw
    right boundary */

/* if the brick hit is on the extreme left
   */
if ( ( BallX + 10 ) / 32 == 0 )
    line ( 0, 0, 0, 50 ) ;  /* redraw left
    boundary */

/* if the brick hit is in the topmost
   layer */
if ( layer == 0 )
    line ( 0, 0, MaxX, 0 ) ;  /* redraw top
    boundary */

/* set appropriate array element to 1 to
   indicate absence of brick */
bri[layer][ ( BallX + 10 ) / 32 ] = 1 ;

BallY = BallY + 1 ;  /* update the y
   coordinate */
dy = -dy ; /* change the current direction
   of the ball */
score += 10 ;  /* increment the score by
   10 */
```

```
        gotoxy ( 16, 25 ) ;
        printf("%d", score);  /* display latest
           score */

        /* if the first brick is hit during a
           throw*/
    }


    /* if ball reached the bottom */
    if ( BallY > 180 - 12 )
    {

        /* if paddle missed the ball */
        if ( BallX < Base1 - 20 || BallX > Base1 +
           50 )
        {
           /* continue the decrement of the ball
           */
           while ( BallY < 177 )
           {
              /* erase the image of the ball at
           the old coordinates */
              putimage ( OldX, OldY, m1, XOR_PUT )
           ;

              /* put the image of the ball at the
           new coordinates */
              putimage ( BallX, BallY, m1, XOR_PUT
           ) ;

              /* introduce delay for fewseconds
           */
              delay ( speed ) ;

              /* saveing current x and y coordinates
           of the ball */
              OldX = BallX ;
              OldY = BallY ;

              /* update ballx and bally to move
```

```
the ball in correct direction */
   BallX = BallX + dx ;
   BallY = BallY + dy ;
}

chance— ; /* decrement the total number
of chances */
score -= 10 ;  /* decrement 10 points
for each ball lost */
gotoxy ( 16, 25 ) ;
printf("%d",score);  /* display latest
score */
bell ( 1 ) ;

/* erase one  of the available balls */
if ( chance )
   putimage ( 515 + ( chance - 1 ) * 35
- 12 , MaxY - 10, m1, XOR_PUT ) ;

/* if the last ball is being played */
if ( chance == 1 )
{
   gotoxy ( 45, 25 ) ;
   printf( "Last ball... careful!");
}

/* if all the balls are lost */
if ( !chance )
{
   gotoxy ( 45, 25 ) ;
   printf("Press any key to continue
...         " );
   outtextxy ( MidX, MidY, "Better luck
next time" ) ;
   bell ( 2 ) ;

   closegraph() ;
   restorecrtmode() ;
   closegraph();      /* Close the
graphics mode */
```

```
        Initialize();      /* Intialize the
     graphics mode */
        setbkcolor(4);
        SayGoodbye();      /* Display the
     That's all Folks message */
        closegraph();      /* Return the
     system to text mode  */
        exit ( 0 ) ;
     }
   }

   /* if ball is collected on paddle */
   bell ( 4 ) ;
   BallY = 180 - 12 ;   /* restore the y
      coordinate of ball */
   dy = -dy ;  /* move the ball upwards */
}

/* put the image of the ball at the old
    coordinates */
putimage ( OldX, OldY, m1, OR_PUT ) ;

/* erase the image of the ball at the old
    coordinates */
putimage ( OldX, OldY, m1, XOR_PUT ) ;

/* put the image of the ball at the upadted
    coordinates */
putimage ( BallX, BallY, m1, XOR_PUT ) ;

/* if all the bricks have been knockout */
if ( score == 500 - ( ( 4 - chance ) * 20 )
    )
{
   outtextxy ( MidX, MidY, "Winner !!" ) ;

   if ( score < 600 )
      outtextxy ( MidX, MidY + 30, "Try to
      score 600" ) ;
   else
      outtextxy ( MidX, MidY + 30, " GREAT!"
```

```
        ) ;

        bell ( 2 ) ;

        closegraph() ;
        restorecrtmode() ;
        exit ( 0 ) ;
    }

    /* introduce delay for few seconds */
    delay ( speed ) ;

    /* if the key is pressed to move the paddle
       */
    if ( kbhit() )
    {
        /* interrupt issue to obtain the ascii
           and scan codes of key hit */
        ii.h.ah = 0 ;
        int86 ( 22, &ii, &oo ) ;

        /* put the image of the paddle at the old
           coordinates */
        putimage ( Base1, Base2, m2, OR_PUT ) ;

        /* erase the image of the paddle at the
           old coordinates */
        putimage ( Base1, Base2, m2, XOR_PUT ) ;

        /* if Esc key has been pressed */
        if ( oo.h.ah == 1 )
           exit ( 0 ) ;

        /* right arrow key */
        if ( oo.h.ah == 75 )
           Base1 = Base1 - 25 ;

        /* left arrow key */
        if ( oo.h.ah == 77 )
```

```
                Base1= Base1 + 25 ;

             /* if paddle goes beyond left boundary */
             if ( Base1 < 0 )
                Base1 = 0 ;

             /* if paddle goes beyond right boundary
                */
             if ( Base1 > 589 )
                Base1 = 589 ;

             /* put the image of the paddle at the
                proper position */
             putimage ( Base1, Base2, m2, XOR_PUT ) ;
          }

       }
       closegraph();
       Initialize();
       SayGoodbye(); /* Give user the closing screen
                */
       closegraph(); /* Return the system to text mode
                */
       return(0);
    }


    /* This function creates the opening screen and
                displyed instruction related to the game
                along with two option play or exit.After
                selecting the paly option it display
                three levels of the game and according
                to your choice you can select any
                level.This selected level is returned
                by this function to the mainprogram
                according to which the speed is assigned
                to the ball*/


    screen()
    {
       int i, j, lx = 0, ly = 0, ch ;

          rectangle(1,1,600,195);
```

```
setbkcolor(4);
/* set the textstyle for displaying
      instruction */
changetextstyle ( DEFAULT_FONT, HORIZ_DIR,
      0 ) ;
outtextxy ( 150, 55, "  Instructions " ) ;
changetextstyle (4, HORIZ_DIR, 5 );
outtextxy ( 130, 0, " B R I C K S" ) ;
changetextstyle ( DEFAULT_FONT, HORIZ_DIR,
      0 ) ;
outtextxy ( 30, 68, "Use left and right
      arrow keys to move paddle." ) ;
outtextxy ( 30, 88, "If you don't collect
      the ball on the paddle, you lose the
      ball." ) ;
outtextxy ( 30, 108, "On loosing a ball you
      loose 20 points." ) ;
outtextxy ( 30, 128, "On taking a brick you
      gain 5 points." ) ;
changetextstyle(7, HORIZ_DIR, 3);
outtextxy ( 100, 148, "Press any key to
      continue ..." ) ;
bell ( 3 ) ;  /* ring music */
fflush ( stdin ) ;
if ( getch() == 0 )
   getch() ;

closegraph();
initgraph ( &graphdriver, &graphmode, "
      d:\turboc3" ) ;
rectangle(2,2,620,195);
setbkcolor(4);
/* display the main menu */
while ( 1 )
{

   changetextstyle(4,HORIZ_DIR,5);
   outtextxy ( 60, 8, "Options Available:" ) ;
   outtextxy ( 150, 55, "Play ( P )" ) ;
   outtextxy ( 150, 125, "Exit ( E )" ) ;
```

```
        ch = 0 ;

        /* continue untill you select the correct
           choice  */
        while ( ! ( ch == 'E' ||   ch == 'P' ) )
        {
           fflush ( stdin ) ;

           /* if a special key is hit, flush the
              keyboard buffer */
           if ( ( ch = getch() ) == 0 )
              getch() ;
           else
              ch = toupper ( ch ) ;     /* store the
              uppercase of the choice made*/
        }

        if ( ch == 'P' )
           break ;
        if (ch == 'E')
           exit ( 0 ) ;

     }

     setviewport ( 1, 125 - 12, MaxX - 1, MaxY - 1,
           1 ) ;
     clearviewport() ;
     closegraph();
     initgraph  ( &graphdriver, &graphmode, "
           d:\turboc3" ) ;
     rectangle(2,2,620,195);
     setbkcolor(4);

     /* display menu for the diffrent levels */
     changetextstyle(7,HORIZ_DIR,3);
     outtextxy ( 60, 8, "Select the level for play:"
           ) ;
     outtextxy ( 150,50, "Slow ( S )" ) ;
     outtextxy ( 150, 100, "Medium ( M )" ) ;
     outtextxy ( 150, 150, "Fast ( F )" ) ;
```

```
    /* accept user's choice */
    fflush ( stdin ) ;
    if ( ( ch = getch() ) == 0 )
        getch() ;

    clearviewport() ;

    /* return the choice selected by the user */
    return ( ch ) ;
}

/* This function draws bricks at the start of the
            game.There are four layers of
the bricks */
bricks()
{
    int i, j, lx = 0, ly = 0 ;

    for ( i = 0 ; i < 5 ; i++ )  /* 5 rows */
    {
        for ( j = 0 ; j < 30 ; j++ )  /* 20 columns
            */
        {
            /* draw a brick at appropriate coordinates
                */
            rectangle ( lx, ly, lx + 20, ly + 7 ) ;
            floodfill ( lx + 1, ly + 1, 2 ) ;

            lx = lx + 32 ;
        }

        lx = 0 ;
        ly = ly + 10 ;
    }
}

/* This function erases the  brick which is knock
            by the ball */
```

```
delbrick ( int b, int l )
{
   /* b - brick number, l - layer */

   setcolor ( BLACK ) ;
   rectangle ( b * 32, l * 10, ( b * 32 ) + 20 , (
         l * 10 ) + 7 ) ;
   rectangle ( b * 32 + 1, l * 10, ( b * 32 ) + 20
         - 1, ( l * 10 ) + 7 - 1 ) ;
   rectangle ( b * 32 + 2, l * 10, ( b * 32 ) + 20
         - 2, ( l * 10 ) + 7 - 2 ) ;
   rectangle ( b * 32 + 3, l * 10, ( b * 32 ) + 20
         - 3, ( l * 10 ) + 7 - 3 ) ;
   rectangle ( b * 32 + 4, l * 10, ( b * 32 ) + 20
         - 4, ( l * 10 ) + 7 - 4 ) ;
   rectangle ( b * 32 + 5, l * 10, ( b * 32 ) + 20
         - 5, ( l * 10 ) + 7 - 5 ) ;
   rectangle ( b * 32 + 6, l * 10, ( b * 32 ) + 20
         - 6, ( l * 10 ) + 7 - 6 ) ;
   setcolor ( CGA_YELLOW ) ;
}

/* plays different types of music */
bell ( int m_no )
{
   /* natural frequencies of 7 notes */
   float wave[6] = { 120.81, 136.83, 144.81, 154.61,
         216, 240 } ;
   int n, i ;

   switch ( m_no )
   {
      case 1 :
         for ( i = 0 ; i < 6 ; i++ )
         {
            sound ( wave[i] * 1 ) ;
            delay ( 30 ) ;
         }
         nosound() ;
         break ;
```

```
case 2 :
   for ( i = 0 ; i < 15 ; i++ )
   {
      n = random ( 6 ) ;
      sound ( wave[n] * 2 ) ;
      delay ( 100 ) ;
   }
   nosound() ;
   break ;

case 3 :
   while ( !kbhit() )
   {
      n = random ( 6 ) ;
      sound ( wave[n] * 2 ) ;
      delay ( 100 ) ;
   }
   nosound() ;

   /* flush the keyboard buffer */
   if ( getch() == 0 )
      getch() ;

   break ;

case 4 :
   for ( i = 5 ; i >= 0 ; i-- )
   {
      sound ( wave[i] * 4 ) ;
      delay ( 15 ) ;
   }
   nosound() ;
   break ;

case 5 :
   sound ( wave[2] * 5 ) ;
   delay ( 50 ) ;
   nosound() ;
```

```
    }
}
/*                              */
/*INITIALIZE: Initializes the graphics system &
          reports*/
/* any errors which occured. */
/*                              */

void Initialize(void)
{
  int xasp, yasp; /* Used to read the aspect
          ratio*/

  GraphDriver = DETECT;    /* Request auto-
          detection */
 initgraph( &GraphDriver, &GraphMode, "d:\turboc3"
          );
  ErrorCode = graphresult();         /*   Read
          result of initialization*/
  if( ErrorCode != grOk ){       /* Error occured
          during init    */
   printf(" Graphics System Error: %s\n",
          grapherrormsg( ErrorCode ) );
   exit( 1 );
  }

  getpalette( &palette ); /* Read the palette
          from board */
  MaxColors = getmaxcolor() + 1;     /*   Read
          maximum number of colors*/

  MaxXX = getmaxx();
  MaxYY = getmaxy();            /* Read size of
          screen */

   getaspectratio( &xasp, &yasp );    /* read the
          hardware aspect */
   AspectRatio = (double)xasp / (double)yasp; /*
          Get correction factor*/

 }
```

```
/*                                                  */
/* SAYGOODBYE: Give a closing screen to the user
            before leaving. */
/*                                                  */

void SayGoodbye(void)
{
  struct viewporttype viewinfo; /* Structure to
            read viewport    */
  int h, w;

  MainWindow( "== Finale ==" );

  getviewsettings( &viewinfo ); /* Read viewport
            settings   */
  changetextstyle( TRIPLEX_FONT, HORIZ_DIR, 4 );
  settextjustify( CENTER_TEXT, CENTER_TEXT );

  h = viewinfo.bottom - viewinfo.top;
  w = viewinfo.right  - viewinfo.left;
  outtextxy( w/2, h/2, "That's all, folks!" );

  StatusLine( "Press any key to EXIT" );
  getch();

  cleardevice();    /* Clear the graphics screen
            */

}

/*                                                  */
/* MAINWINDOW: Establish the main window for the
            demo and set      */
/* a viewport for the demo code.
            */
/*                                                  */

void MainWindow( char *header )
{
  int height;
```

```
  cleardevice();             /* Clear graphics
          screen */
  setcolor( MaxColors - 1 );           /*     Set
          current color to white     */
  setviewport( 0, 0, MaxXX, MaxYY, 1 );    /    *
          Open port to full screen   */

 height = textheight("H"); /*Get basic text height
          */

  changetextstyle( DEFAULT_FONT, HORIZ_DIR, 1 );
  settextjustify( CENTER_TEXT, TOP_TEXT );
  outtextxy( MaxXX/2, 2, header );
 setviewport(0, height+4, MaxXX, MaxYY-(height+4),
          1);
  DrawBorder();
   setviewport(1, height+5, MaxXX-1, MaxYY-
          (height+5),1);

}

/*                            */
/* STATUSLINE: Display a status line at the bottom
          of the screen.  */
/*                            */

void StatusLine( char *msg )
{
  int height;

  setviewport( 0, 0, MaxXX, MaxYY, 1 );    /    *
          Open port to full screen   */
  setcolor( MaxColors - 1 );           /*     Set
          current color to white     */

  changetextstyle( DEFAULT_FONT, HORIZ_DIR, 1 );
  settextjustify( CENTER_TEXT, TOP_TEXT );
  setlinestyle( SOLID_LINE, 0, NORM_WIDTH );
  setfillstyle( EMPTY_FILL, 0 );
```

```
height = textheight( "H" );          /* Detemine
         current height       */
bar( 0, MaxYY-(height+4), MaxXX, MaxYY );
rectangle( 0, MaxYY-(height+4), MaxXX, MaxYY );
outtextxy( MaxXX/2, MaxYY-(height+2), msg );
setviewport(1, height+5, MaxXX-1, MaxYY-
         (height+5),1);

}

/*                                          */
/* DRAWBORDER: Draw a solid single line around
         the current                        */
/* viewport.                                */
/*                                          */

void DrawBorder(void)
{
  struct viewporttype vp;

  setcolor( MaxColors - 1 );          /*    Set
         current color to white       */

  setlinestyle( SOLID_LINE, 0, NORM_WIDTH );

  getviewsettings( &vp );
  rectangle( 0, 0, vp.right-vp.left, vp.bottom-
         vp.top );

}

/*                                          */
/* CHANGETEXTSTYLE: similar to settextstyle, but
         checks for */
/* errors that might occur while loading the font
         file.   */
/*                                          */

void changetextstyle(int font, int direction, int
         charsize)
{
```

```
int ErrorCode;

graphresult();                    /* clear error code */
settextstyle(font, direction, charsize);
ErrorCode = graphresult();     /* check result
        */
if( ErrorCode != grOk ){ /* if error occured */
 closegraph();
 printf(" Graphics System Error: %s\n",
        grapherrormsg( ErrorCode ) );
 exit( 1 );
}
}

/* The main function body of main screen which
        displays the main screen creating the
        opening screen display */
mainscreen()
{
  int maxx, maxy, in, area;

  // get maximum x, y coordinates of the screen
  maxx = getmaxx();
  maxy = getmaxy();

  // setbkcolor sets the current background color
        using the palette
  setbkcolor(RED);

  // Draws a rectangle (graphics mode)
  rectangle(0, 0, maxx, maxy);

  // sets the line style and text justification
        in screen
  changetextstyle(1, HORIZ_DIR, 0);

  // displaying the output text on main screen
  outtextxy(220, 20, "WELCOME");
  outtextxy(240,60,"   TO ");
  outtextxy(220,100," BRICKS");
```

```
    changetextstyle(7, HORIZ_DIR, 3);
    bell(3);
    outtextxy(110, 150,"Press any key to
         continue...");

    // Flushes the standard input device
    fflush(stdin);
    getch();
    closegraph();

}
```

Write' a 'C' program to convert polar co-ordinates to Cartesian co-ordinates and vice versa.

```
#include<stdio.h>
#include<math.h>
int main(int argc,char*argv[] )
{
int radius, theta;
int x,y;
int choice;
printf ( "1. \tPolar to Cartesian conversion\n" )
          ;
printf("2.\t Cartesian to Polar conversion\n")
printf("Enter choice:") ;
scanf ( "%d" , &choice)
if choice==1)
{
printf ( "Enter the radius r:");
scanf("%d",&radius);
printf ( "Enter the angle theta:");
scanf ( "%d", &theta) ;
x=radius*cos(theta)
y=radius*sin(theta)
printf ( "Cartesian form in x+iy:");
printf("%2f+%.2fi", x,y) ;
}
else if (choice==2)
{
```

```
printf ("Enter the value of x:") ;
scanf ( "%d" , &x) ;
 printf("Enter the value of y:");
scanf ( "%d" , &y) ;
radius=sqrt (((x*x) +(y*y))) ;
theta=atan({y/x);
printf ( "Polar form {r, q) : " ) ;
printf ( " ( %.2 f , %.2 f ) " , r, theta) ;
}
return0;
}
```

Write a 'C' program to find out the maximum and minimum of three integers read as input.

```
#include<stdio.h>
int main(int argc, char*argv[ ])
{
int a[3] ;
printf("Enter the first number:");
scanf("%d", &a[0] ) ;
printf ( "Enter the second number: ") ;
scanf ( "%d" &a [1] ) ;
printf ( "Enter the third number: " ) ;
scanf ("%d" &a [2] ) ;
if(a[0]>a[1])
{
if(a[0]>a[2])
{
printf ( 'The first' number%d is the largest", a [
          0] ) ;
if(a[1]>a[2])
printf ( "The third number %d is the smallest" ,
          a[2] ) ;
else
printf ( "The second number %d is the smallest",
          a[1]) ;
}
else
```

```
{
printf("The third number %d is the largest", a[2]
printf ( "The second number %d is the smallest"
        a[1]);
}
}
else
{
if(a[1]>a[2])
{
printf ( "The second number %d is the largest" ,
a[1])  ;if(a[0]>a[2])
printf ( "The third number %d is the smallest"
a[2]);
else
printf ( "The first number %d is the smallest",
        a[0] ) ;
}
else
{
printf ( "The third number %d is the largest" ,
        a[2] ) ;
printf ( "The first number %d is the smallest" ,
        a[0]) ;
}
}
return 0;
}
```

Write a 'C'program to read an integer 'n' and print whether 'n' is a prime number or not:

```
#include<stdio.h>
#include<math.h>
int main(int argc char* argv [ ] )
{
int n,i;
printf("Enter the number;");
scanf("%d",&n) ;
for(i=2;i<n;i++)
```

```
{
if (n%i) ==0 )
{
printf("\n%d is NOT a prime nurnber",n) ;
return 0;
}
}
printf ( " \n%d is a prime number" , n)
return0;
}
```

Write a 'C' program to read an array of 'n' numbers and to sort an array using selection sort algorithm.

```
#include<stdio.h>
#include<math.h>
#define ARRAY_SIZE 10
void selection_sort(intx[ ], int lim)
{
inti, eff_size, maxpos, tmp;
for (eff_size=lim; eff_size>1;eff_size– )
{
maxpos=0;
for(i=0;i<eff_size;i++)
maxpos=x[i]>x[maxpos]? i:maxpos;
tmp=x[maxpos];
x[maxpos]=x[eff-size-1];
x[eff_size-1]=tmp;
}
}
int main(int argc, char* argv [ ] )
{
int x[ARRAY_SIZE];
int i;
for(1=0;i<10;i++)
{
printf ("Enter%dnumber;",i+1)
scanf { "%d", &x [ i] ) ;
}
```

```
selection_sort(x, ARRAY_SIZE) ;
printf ( "\nSorted array" );
for(i=0;i<10;i++)
printf("%d",x[i]) ;
return 0;
}
```

Consider a matrix of 0's and 1's. A sequence of successive 1's along a row or a column or a diagonal is defined to be a line. The number of 1's in a line is called a length. Write 'C' program to find out the line with the maximum length in, such a matrix.

```
#include<stdio.h>
in matrix[3] [3] ;
int inrow()
{
int count[3]={0}, i, j, len;
for(i=0;i<3;i++)
{
for(j=0;j<3;j++ )
if(j!=0)
{
if(matrix[i] [j-1]==1&& matrix[i] [j]==1)
count[i]+=1;
}
if(count[i]==2)count[i]+-1;
}
len=count[0]>count[1]?count[0] :count[1];
len=count[2J>len?count[2] :len;
return len;
}
int incol()
{
int count [3] ={0} , i, j , len;
for(i=0;i<3;i++)
{
for(j=0;j<3;j++ )
if(j !=0)
{
```

```
if(matrix[j-1] [i]==1&& matrix[j] [I]==1)
count[i]+=1;
}
if (count [i] ==2) count [i] +=1;
}
len=count[0]>count[1]?count[0] :count[1];
len=count[2]>len?countt2] :len;
return len;
}
int diagonal()
{
int i, j , len=0 ;
for(i=1;i<3;i++)
if(matrix[i] [i]==1&& matrix[i-1] [i-1]==1)len+=1;
if(len!=3)
{
for(i=0;i<3;i++)
for(j=0;j<3;j++
{
if(matrix[i] [j]==1}
{
if(i+1<3&&j+1<3)
if(matrix[i+1] [j+1]==1)len=2;
if(i+1<3&&j-1<3}
if (matrix [ i+1 ] [ j -1] ==1} len=2 ;
if(i-1<3&&j+1<3)
if(matrix[i-1] [j+1]==1)len=2;
if(i-1<3&&j-1<3)
if(matrix[i-1]Ij-1]==1}len=2;
}
}
return len;
}
int main (void) {
int i,j, length = 0, rowlen, collen, dialen;
printf("enter the elements of the matrix\n") ;
for(i=0;i<3;i++)
{
```

```
printf("enter next row") ;
for(j=0;j<3;j++)
scanf("%d", &matrix[i] [j]);
}
rowlen=inrow();
collen=incol(); ,
dialen=diagonal();
length=rowlen>c,ollen?rowlen:colleen;
length=length>dialen?length:dialen;
printf("the maximum length of the line=%d", length);
}
```

Write a recursive 'C' function to compute the greatest common divisor of two positive integers

---

```
#include<stdio.h>
public  static  long  greatest  Conunon
          Divisor(longp,longq)
{
intr;
//p must be greater than q
if(p<q)
{
return greatest Common Divisor(q,p);
}
r=p%q;
if(r==0)
{
return q;
}//else
return greatestCommonDivisor(q,r);
}
int main (void}
{
intp,q;
printf("Enter the first number;");
scanf ( "%d" , &p) ;
printf ( "Enter the second number; ") ;
scanf ( "d", &q) ;
```

```
printf ( "The GCD of the two numbers is: %d",
            greatest Common Divisor (p, q) ) ;
return 0
}
```

Define a structure for a student having name, roll number and marks obtained in six subject. Assume that "allStudents" is an array of students. Write 'C' functions to:

(a) print the name and roll number of the students who ha ye secured highest marks in each subject

(b) print the name and roll number of the student who has secured highest total marks. Write a 'C' program to read details of 'n' students and call the above functions to generate a report

```
#include<stdio.h>
#define TOTAL_SUBJECTS 6
struct student
{
char name[25];
int rollno;
unsigned int marks[TOTAL_SUBJECTS];
}allStudents[20];
void PrintSubjectWiseHighest(int n)
{
inti, j ;
int max:pos=0;
for(i=0;i<TOTAL_SUBJECTS;i++)
{
maxpos=0;
for ( j =0; j <n; j++)
maxpos=allStudents[j].marks [i] >allStudents
            [maxpos].marks[i]?j:maxpos;
printf("%s(%d) has scored the highest mark of %d
            in subject
%d\n",allStudents[maxpos].name,allStudents[maxpos},rollno,
            allStudents[maxpos].marks[i],i+1);
}
}
void PrintTotalHighest(int n)
{
```

```
inti,j;
int maxpos=0;
int total=0;
intmaxtotal=0
maxpos=0;
maxtotal=0;
for(i=0;i<n;i++)
{
total=0;
for(j=0;j<TOTAL_SUBJECTS;j++)
total+=allStudents[i].marks[j];
if(maxtotal<total)
{
maxtotal=total; maxpos=I;
}
}
printf("%s(%d) has scored the total highest mark
          of %d in allsubjects\n",
          allStudents[maxpos].name,
          allStudents[maxpos].rollno,maxtotal);
}
}
int main(void)
of %d
{
int n;
int i, j;
printf ( "Enter total number of students: ");
scanf ( "%d", &n) ;
for(i=0;i<n;i++)
{
printf ( "Name: " )
gets(allStudents[I].name) ;
printf ( "Roll Number: " ) ;
scanf ( "%d", &allStudents [ i].rollno );
for(j=0;j<n;j++)
{
printf("%d subject marks",j+1);
```

```
scanf("%d",&allStudents[i] .marks[j]);
}
}
PrintSubjectWiseHighest(n);
PrintTotalHighest(n);
return0;
}
```

Write a 'C' function to insert a number properly into the already sorted linked list of numbers. Use this function repeatedly to sort a series of numbers provided at the input

```
#include<stdio.h>
struct list
{
int n;
struct list* next;
} ;
void InsertlntoList(struct list**head,int n)
{
struct list *trav=NULL;
Struct list *tmp=*head;
struct list *node=malloc(sizeof(struct list));
node->n=n;
node->next=NULL;
/* First time when a node is inserted */
if( (*head) ==NULL)
{
{*head) =node;
return;
}
/* When the input element is less than the first
          element itself */
if(n<(*head)->n)
{
(*head} =node;
(*head}->next=tmp;
return;
/* Traverse through the list till the appropriate
          position is found. */
```

```
trav=*head;
while ((trav->next!=NULL)&&(trav->n<n))
{
tmp=trav;
trav=trav->next;
}
/* Conditions for inserting into the middle of
        the list */
if((trav->next!=NULL)    II    ((trav-
        >next==NULL)&&(trav->n>n)))
{
tmp->next=node;
nocte->next=trav;
return;
}
/* Inserting/appending into the end of the list
        */
trav->next=node;
return;
}
int main{void}
struct list *head=NULL;
int ch='y';
int n;
while(ch=='y'||ch=='y')
{
printf("Enter number;");
scanf ( "%d", &n) ;
InsertlntoList(&head,n);
printf ( "Do you want to continue inserting (y/
        n):");
scanf("%c",&ch) ;
}
return 0;
}
```

Define a self referential structure for representing a simple linked list of integers Write a 'C; function to split the list into two lists so that the first list contains all even numbered elements and the second list contans all Odd numbered elements. For example, it the original list is {2,8, 1, 14,6,18,0,17} then the resultant first list would be {8, 1~ 18, 17} and the second list would be {2,1,0}.

```
#include<stdio.h>
struct list
{
int num;
struct list *next
};
int main(void)
{
struct list *list1=NULL,*list2=NULL,*list3=NULL;
int num=0,i,ele=0;
struct list *temp=list1,*node,*temp1,*temp2; printf
          ( "enter number of element: " ) ;
scanf("%d",&num);
printf ( "enter elements to enter\n" ) ;
for(i=0;i<num;i++)
{
scant ( " %d", &ele) ;
node=(struct list*)malloc(sizeot(struct list) node-
          >num=ele;
node->next=NULL;
it(temp==NULL)
{
list1=node;
temp=node;
}
else
temp->next=node;
temp=node;
}
temp=list1;
temp1=list2;
temp2=list3;
for(i=0;i<num;i+=2)
{
if (temp! =NULL)
```

```
{
node=(struct list*) malloc\sizeof(struct list));

node->next=NULL;
node->num=temp->num;
if(temp2==NULL)
{
list2=node;
temp1=node;
}
else
temp1->next=node;
temp1=node;
temp=temp->next;
}
if (temp! =NULL)
{
node=(struct list*) malloc(sizeof(struct list));
node->next=NULL;
node->num=temp->num;
if(temp2==NULL)
{
list3=node;
temp2=node;
}
else
temp2->next=node ;
temp2=node;
temp=temp->next;
}
}
temp1=list2;
temp2=list3;
while(temp1!=NULL)
{
printf { "list! : %d\n" , temp1->num) ;
temp1=temp1->next;
}
```

```
while(temp2!'=NULL)
{
printf("list2:%d\n",temp2->num);
temp2=temp2->next;
}
}
```

Write 'C' function to

(a) copy the content of one file to another

(b)count the number of words in a file; Assume that a word is a sequence of letters ending with a blank or a tab or an end of line marker or end of file or punctuation symbols such as ",", ".", "!" and "?".

Write a 'C' program to open a file and can the above functions to count the number of words in that file.

```
#include<stdio.h>
void copyfile(FILE* dest, FILE* src
{
char str;
while (!feof(src))
{
str=fgetc(src)
fptc(str,dest);
}
}
void count(FILE* src)
{
char c,prev;
int count=0;
int flag=0;
while ( ! feof (src) )
{
c=fgetc(src);
if(c=='\n'l| c=''|| feof(src) ||c=='\t' ||c=='.'
          ||c==','++c=='!'||c=='?')
{
if(flag==0)
{
```

```
count++
}
flag=1;
}
else
flag=0
}
printf ( "number of words=%d", count);
}
int main{void
FILE*fp, *fp1;
fp=fopen("c:\\one.txt", "r+");
fp1=fopen ( "c : \\two.txt" , "r+");
copyfile(fp,fp1) ;
fp1=fopen ( "c : \\two. txt" , "r+" );
count(fp1);
}
```

12 Questions

You do not have to pay to get this program, it is part of the HTML group or can be downloaded free.

Answer the Following Questions

Chapter 1 — Introduction to C

1. Describe the process of learning C.
2. Describe the following terms with reference to C:

   Constants
   Primary Constants
   Character Constants
   Integer Constants
   Real Contstants
   Secondary Constants
   Variables

3. Describe the various arithmetic statements.

Chapter 2 — Structures in C

1. Describe various decision control structures.
2. Describe various loop control sturctures.
3. Describe the various case control structures.

Chapter 3 — Functions and Pointers in C

1. Describe the various type of functions available in C.
2. What do you understand by pointers in C?
3. Which are the various type of pointers?
4. Describe the various type of memory models in C.

Chapter 4 — Arrays in C

1. Describe the variou type of Arrays in C.
2. Describe how would you do the following:

   Declare an Array
   Access Array Elements
   Enter Data into an Array
   Read Data from an Array
   Check the bounds
   Pass Elements to a Function

Chapter 5 — Strings in C

1. Describe the various library strings.

2. Describe the working of followins strings:

strcpy strcmp

Chapter 6 — Input Output Operations in C

1. Describe the various type of Input Output operations in C.
2. Describe the various escape functions.
3. Describe the working of following functions:

   scanf() sprintf()

   sscanf() gets()

   puts()
4. Describe how would you do the following?

   Open a file Read from a file

   Close a file Write to a file

Chapter 7 — Library Functions

1. Describe the various functions under the following categories.

   Mathematical Functions String Functions

   Character Classification Macros

   File Handling Functions Directory Control Functions

   Macros Graphics Functions

   Time and Date Related Functions

   Miscellaneous Functions

Chapter 8 — Unions, Stacks, Links and Queues

1. What are Unions?
2. Describe the various Unions in C.
3. What are Stacks?
4. What are Links?
5. What are Queues?

Chapter 9 — File Processing and Pre Process Directives

1. Describe the various file accessing functions in C.
2. Describe the various file manipulation functions.
3. Describe the various pre processor directives.

Chapter 10 — Tubro C

1. Describe the various items of the menus of Turbo C.
2. Describe the various hot keys.

Other Titles in Learning Series

1. Windows 98
2. Word 2000
3. PageMaker 6.5
4. Excel 2000
5. Access 2000
6. CorelDRAW 9
7. PowerPoint 2000
8. Outlook 2000
9. FrontPage 2000
10. MS Office 2000
11. Photoshop 5.5
12. Internet and e-mail
13. Flash 4
14. HTML 4
15. C++
16. DOS 6.0/6.22
17. Visual FoxPro
18. e-commerce
19. JAVA
20. JAVA Servlets
21. Windows ME
22. UNIX
23. JavaScript
24. Visual Basic 6.0
25. Tally 5.4
26. AutoCAD 2000
27. XML/XHTML
28. Flash 5.0
29. Photoshop 6.0
30. Oracle 8i
31. CorelDRAW 10
32. Word 2002
33. Excel 2002
34. Access 2002
35. PowerPoint 2002
36. FrontPage 2002
37. Microsoft Office XP
38. C#
39. Computer Fundamentals
40. C
41. Dreamweaver 4.0
42. Red Hat Linux 7.1
43. Windows XP
44. Tally 6.3
45. Simple Networking
46. HTML (Rev.)
47. Photoshop 6 (Rev.)
48. PageMaker 7.0
49. Illustrator 9.0
50. Flash 5 (Rev.)
51. SQL Programming
52. JavaScript (Rev.)
53. Multimedia
54. PC Hardware
55. Internet & e-mail (Rev.)
56. Unix (Rev.)
57. C++ (Rev.)
58. MS Office 2000 (Rev.)
59. Visual Basic (Rev.)
60. Java 2 (Rev.)
61. Visual FoxPro (Rev.)
62. Photoshop 7
63. Illustrator 10
64. Visual C++
65. AutoCAD 2002
66. Microsoft Office XP (Rev.)
67. Flash MX
68. Oracle 9i
69. CorelDRAW 11
70. Linux 8
71. 3d Max 5.0
72. MCQ in Unix

73. MCQ in C++
74. MCQ in C
75. Microsoft Office 2003
76. Microsoft Office Word 2003
77. Microsoft Office Excel 2003
78. AutoCAD 2004
79. DreamWeaver MX 2004
80. Flash MX 2004
81. MS Office Access 2003
82. MS Office FrontPage 2003
83. MS Office PowerPoint 2003
84. CorelDRAW 12
85. Photoshop 2004 CS
86. AutoCAD 2005
87. Tally 7.2
88. Computer Fundamentals (New Format)
89. HTML 4 (New Format)
90. Microsoft Office 2003 (New Format)
91. CorelDRAW 12 (New Format)
92. Photoshop CS 2004 (New Format)
93. Internet and e-mail (New Format)
94. JavaScript (New Format)
95. e-commerce (Revised and New Format)
96. Windows XP (New Format)
97. C (Revised and New Format)

CHAPTER 12

Questions

Introduction

Questions are there to test your knowledge about the subject which has been taught in the preceeding chapters.

Answer the Following Questions

OBJECTIVE TYPE QUESTIONS

1. A Horizontal Rule is the part of:
   (a) Common Objects (b) Layout Category
   (c) Forms Category (d) Data Category.
2. Table is part of:
   (a) Common Objects (b) Layout Category
   (c) Forms Category (d) Data Category.
3. Label is part of:
   (a) Common Objects (b) Layout Category
   (c) Forms Category (d) Data Category.
4. Recordset Paging is part of:.
   (a) Common Objects (b) Layout Category
   (c) Forms Category (d) Data Category.
5. Comment is part of:
   (a) Common Objects (b) Layout Category
   (c) Forms Category (d) Data Category.
6. Expanded Tables Mode is part of:
   (a) Common Objects (b) Layout Category
   (c) Forms Category (d) Data Category.
7. Radio buttons are part of:
   (a) Common Objects (b) Layout Category
   (c) Forms Category (d) Data Category.
8. Delete Record is part of:
   (a) Common Objects (b) Layout Category
   (c) Forms Category (d) Data Category.
9. No Script is part of:
   (a) Common Objects (b) Layout Category
   (c) Forms Category (d) Data Category.
10. Spray Tabbed Panels is part of:
    (a) Common Objects (b) Layout Category
    (c) Forms Category (d) Data Category.
11. Spry Validation Checkbox is part of:
    (a) Common Objects (b) Layout Category
    (c) Forms Category (d) Data Category.

12. Dynamic Data is part of::
   (a) Common Objects (b) Layout Category
   (c) Forms Category (d) Data Category.
13. Draw Rectangle Hotspot is part of:
   (a) Common Objects (b) Layout Category
   (c) Forms Category (d) Data Category.
14. Spry Menubar Is part of:
   (a) Spry Category (b) Text Category
   (c) Forms Category (d) Data Category.
15. Block Quote is part of:
   (a) Spry Category (b) Text Category
   (c) Forms Category (d) Data Category.
16. Spry Accordion is part of:
   (a) Spry Category (b) Text Category
   (c) Forms Category (d) Data Category.
17. Em-dash is part of:
   (a) Spry Category (b) Text Category
   (c) Forms Category (d) Data Category.
18. Spry Tabbed Panels is part of:
   (a) Spry Category (b) Text Category
   (c) Forms Category (d) Data Category.
19. Definition List is part of:
   (a) Spry Category (b) Text Category
   (c) Forms Category (d) Data Category.
20. For clearning the data from the screen, we use ________ key.
   (a) Delete (b) Ctrl + C
   (c) Ctrl + W (d) Enter.
21. For closing the open file, we use:
   (a) Delete (b) Ctrl + C
   (c) Ctrl + W (d) Enter.
22. For copying the data, we use:
   (a) Delete (b) Ctrl + C
   (c) Ctrl + W (d) Enter.
23. To create a new paragraph, we use:
   (a) Delete (b) Ctrl + C
   (c) Ctrl + W (d) Enter.

24. For cutting the selected data or object, we use:
    (a) Cut (b) Ctrl + Q
    (c) Ctrl + F (d) Ctrl + B
25. To exit or quit, we use:
    (a) Cut (b) Ctrl + Q
    (c) Ctrl + F (d) Ctrl + B
26. To find the next word, we use:
    (a) Cut (b) Ctrl + Q
    (c) Ctrl + F (d) Ctrl + B
27. To make the selected text Bold, we use:
    (a) Cut (b) Ctrl + Q
    (c) Ctrl + F (d) Ctrl + B
28. To make the text italics, we use:
    (a) Ctrl + I (b) Shift + F4
    (c) End (d) Page Down
29. To minimize all windows, use the key-combination of:
    (a) Ctrl + I (b) Shift + F4
    (c) End (d) Page Down
30. To move to the end of the line, use the key-combination of:
    (a) Ctrl + I (b) Shift + F4
    (c) End (d) Page Down
31. To move the page down, use the key-combination of:
    (a) Ctrl + I (b) Shift + F4
    (c) End (d) Page Down
32. To move to page up. use ________ key.
    (a) Page Up (b) Home
    (c) Tab (d) Ctrl + N.
33. To move to start of a line, use the ________ key.
    (a) Page Up (b) Home
    (c) Tab (d) Ctrl + N.
34. To move the next cell, we use the ______ key.
    (a) Page Up (b) Home
    (c) Tab (d) Ctrl + N.
35. To create a new document, we use:
    (a) Page Up (b) Home
    (c) Tab (d) Ctrl + N.

36. For opening an existing document file, we use:
    (a) Ctrl + O (b) Ctrl + Shift + S
    (c) Ctrl + S (d) Double Click
37. To Save As a file, we use:
    (a) Ctrl + O (b) Ctrl + Shift + S
    (c) Ctrl + S (d) Double Click
38. To Save a file, we use:
    (a) Ctrl + O (b) Ctrl + Shift + S
    (c) Ctrl + S (d) Double Click
39. To select a word, we use:
    (a) Ctrl + O (b) Ctrl + Shift + S
    (c) Ctrl + S (d) Double Click
40. To Select All items on the screen, we use:
    (a) Ctrl + A (b) Ctrl + Shift + Left Arrow
    (c) Ctrl + Shift + Right Arrow (d) Ctrl + +(Plus)
41. To Select word on the left, we use::
    (a) Ctrl + A (b) Ctrl + Shift + Left Arrow
    (c) Ctrl + Shift + Right Arrow (d) Ctrl + +(Plus)
42. To Select word on the right, use the key-combination of:
    (a) Ctrl + A (b) Ctrl + Shift + Left Arrow
    (c) Ctrl + Shift + Right Arrow (d) Ctrl + +(Plus)
43. To Zoom in site map, use the key-combination of:
    (a) Ctrl + A (b) Ctrl + Shift + Left Arrow
    (c) Ctrl + Shift + Right Arrow (d) Ctrl + +(Plus)

ANSWERS TO OBJECTIVE TYPE QUESTIONS

1. a	2. b	3. c	4. d
5. a	6. b	7. c	8. d
9. a	10. b	11. c	12. d
13. a	14. a	15. b	16. c
17. d	18. a	19. b	20. a
21. c	22. b	23. d	24. a
25. b	26. c	27. d	28. a
29. b	30. c	31. d	32. a
33. b	34. c	35. d	36. a
37. b	38. c	39. d	40. a
41. b	42. c	43. d	

SUBJECTIVE TYPE QUESTIONS

Chapter 1 Introduction to Dreamweaver CS5

1. Describe the new additions to the version CS5 of Dreamweaver.
2. How would you start Dreamweaver CS5?
3. Describe the various options of toolbar.
4. Describe the various options of statusbar.
5. Describe the various options of Property Inspector.
6. Which are the buttons on the Object Panels?
7. Describe the various options of following panels:
   - Common Objects
   - Layout Objects
   - Forms objects
   - Text
   - HTML
8. How would you customize Dreamweaver for you?

Chapter 2 Creating a New Page in Dreamweaver CS5

1. How would you create a new page?
2. What steps would you take to see your page in the browser?
3. How would add text to your page?
4. Describe the process of adding a line in the page.
5. How would you do the following:
   - Create Unordered List
   - Create Ordered List
   - Change Font
   - Add New Font
   - Make Text Bold/Italics
   - Change Colour of the Text
   - Create a New CSS Style
   - Change a New CSS Style

Chapter 3 Adding Graphics and Multimedia in DreamWeaver CS5

1. Describe the process of doing the following:
   - Adding an Image
   - Adding a Border to an Image
   - Resizinng the Image
   - Changing Dimensions by Dragging
   - Wrapping Text around Image
   - Adding Horizontal Rule.
   - Adding Background Image
   - Adding Multimedia Files
   - Add a Sound File
   - Inserting a Plugin object
   - Adding Looping to the Sound
   - Creating Flash Text
   - Creating a Flash Button
   - Inserting a Java Applet
   - Inserting applet into a Web page
   - Downloading Plugins
   - Adding Flash Files

Chapter 4 Working with Tables in Dreamweaver CS5

1. How would you insert a table in your web page?

2. Describe how would you do the following:
   - Insert a Table within a Table
   - Insert Image in a Table
   - Split a Table Cell
   - Design Your Page Layout Using Tables
   - Create a page layout
   - Turn on Autostretch
   - Turn Your Table into Layers
   - Change Background Colour of a Table
   - Insert Rows or Columns in a Table
   - Merge Cells of a Table
   - Add a Layout Table and Layout cells
   - Use Autostretch to Fit the Page
   - Align Table Cell Content

Chapter 5 Working with Forms in Dreamweaver CS5

1. How would you do the following:
   - Create a Form
   - Add Text Fields
   - Add Labels
   - Add Check Boxes
   - Create a list
   - Add submit and Reset Buttons
   - Add a generic Button
   - Validate the Form
   - Add a Form
   - Apply Text Field Attributes
   - Add Radio Buttons
   - Add a List of Menu
   - Add Push Buttons and Picture Buttons
   - Add an Image Field to Submit a Form
   - Create a Jump Menu

Chapter 6 Working with Frames in Dreamweaver CS5

1. Describe how you would do the following?
   - Dividing a Page into Frames
   - Adding Contents to Frames
   - Saving Frames Pages
   - Naming Frames
   - Hyperlinking to a Frame
   - Setting Frame Borders
   - Adding Noframes Content
   - Viewing Library Items
   - Inserting a Frameset
   - Adding New Content to a Frame
   - Saving the Frameset
   - Deleting Frames
   - Changing Frame Dimensions
   - Turning off the Borders
   - Nesting Page Frames
   - Viewing Templates

Chapter 7 Working with Style Sheets and Layers in Dreamweaver CS5

1. Describe how would you do the following?
   - Create a HTML Tag
   - Apply a Class
   - Use CSS selectors to Modify Links
   - Create a Layer
   - Reposition a Layer
   - Change the Stacking Order of Layers
   - Create a Class
   - Edit a Style Sheet Class
   - Create an External Style Sheet
   - Resize a Layer
   - Add a Background Color to a Layer

Chapter 8 Creating and Applying Templates in Dreamweaver CS5

1. How would you do the following?

Create a Template	Use the Template Category of the Asset Panel
Create a template from an Existing Web page	Create a Template from Scratch
Make an Existing Region Editable	Make a New Editable Region
Apply a Template to a Web Page	Make Changes to a Template
Update Pages That Contain the Template	Use Behaviours, Styles and Timelines in Templates

Chapter 9 More Commands of Dreamweaver CS5

1. How would you create a Custom Snippet?
2. Describe the process of Editing the Keyboard Shortcuts.
3. Describe the process of Using Third Party Extensions.
4. How would you share searches in Dreamweaver CS5?
5. How would you make a menu command?

NOTES

NOTES